Eve:

Always follow your GPS!

In faith,

Uncommon Faith

FELICIA McQUAID

Praise for Uncommon Faith:

"Felicia McQuaid's *Uncommon Faith* provides a tangible definition and practice of faith that even those of us who are mere mortals can understand and therefore participate in this journey of healing and well-being. By creating moments of such eye-opening wonder while connecting to the concrete foundation of her narrative from suffering to enlightenment, *Uncommon Faith* will benefit all readers, whether you are a Buddhist, a yogi, an energy worker, an abuse or trauma survivor, or someone interested in broadening one's healing path.

Using the story of her difficult childhood as a backdrop, Felicia creates a manual for using uncommon faith as the basis of living a balanced and successful life. She provides lesson plans for each reader to follow so that he or she can join Felicia on this expedition to healthier, happier living. *Uncommon Faith* touches upon the subjects of feeling angry, lost or without purpose and coming out the other side with understanding that these hardships are stepping stones to our own greatness. This book is a beautiful read for anyone who is ready to take a leap and step onto the road of uncommon faith toward inner bliss."

Melanie Summers, yoga instructor, Reiki Master Teacher, and fellow survivor

"This powerful and timely book will change the world by changing every single person who reads and receives its message. *Uncommon Faith* breaches the boundaries of limitations. It gives its readers wings, and then carries them to the edge of understanding where, without hesitation, they fly."

Laura Tyree, owner Dragonfly Yoga, Reiki Master Teacher

"In *Uncommon Faith*, Felicia McQuaid harnesses the power of vulnerability to weave her story into the tapestry of faith, hope and love.

As I traveled with Felicia on her journey, her eloquent depiction allowed me to feel the depth of pain in her lows and astronomical celebration of her victories. Felicia's relatability, honest dialogue, brilliant storytelling and insights on the power of faith will inspire you to examine your life and embrace uncommon faith.

Uncommon Faith will be revisited from your bookshelf many times at different stages in your life. It is a must read and a timeless addition to your library."

Melissa L. Strawser, Certified Professional Coach, Reiki Master Teacher & Chief Creative Officer, La Belle Luce, LLC

Disclaimer:

The author tried to recreate events, locales and conversations from her memories of them. In order to maintain anonymity in some instances, the author changed the name of individuals and places. The intent of the author is only to offer information of a general nature to help you in your quest for emotional and spiritual well-being. In the event you use any of the information in this book for yourself, which is your constitutional rights, the author and publisher assume no responsibility for your actions. This book is not intended as a substitute for the medical advice of physicians. The reader should regularly consult a physician in matters relating to his/her health and particularly with respect to any symptoms that may require diagnosis or medical attention.

Credits:

Published by Felicia McQuaid

Edited by Lena Anani & John Hansen

Cover Design by Jenelle Conner

Book Layout by Courtney Ayers

Front Cover Photograph by John Watson: "Road to Heaven"

Author Photograph by Jack Gardner

CD Photography by Jessica Cuadra

Printed in the United States of America

First Printing, 2015

ISBN-13: 978-0692369548

ISBN-10: 0692369546

With faith all things are possible. ⟆

Uncommon Faith Meditations
Available for Purchase

*Listen as Felicia guides you through
each meditation in the book.*

Getting in touch with:
Bonus Track: Faith Poem

1. Faith
2. What am I here for
3. How do you feel
4. Who am I
5. Your G.P.S.
6. Your story
7. The power of faith
8. Energy
9. Openness
10. Present moment
11. Heart
12. Loving kindness
13. What is faith
14. Uncommon faith

Purchase at: Uncommonfaithbook.com

Contents Page

Acknowledgements

"If the only prayer you ever said in your whole life was 'thank you', that would be suffice." Meister Eckhart

I am eternally thankful to my family for their faith in me. To my daughter, Rachel, for always being a shining light of God's grace in my life. To my son, Jonah, for being a powerful force of love in my life and always loving me above all other things. I am eternally thankful to my husband, who has uncommon faith in me and showed me there was another way to live, a way of living that included love, support and happiness. Through this love and support I have been allowed to become all I was meant to be. I have been allowed to grow and explore what it means to have faith in myself. I have been supported in ways I had never known before and through that have created a life of happiness and purpose. Thank you ... Thank you ...

In addition to my family, I must also thank Laura Tyree, my first "official" teacher on this journey. Thank you for seeing in me what I did not yet see and then skillfully drawing it to the surface! You are my teacher, my friend, my soul sister!

To my beautiful friend and divine being, Jenelle Conner, for inspiring me to think bigger and reach for the stars!

To all those I know and do not know who love me and have faith in my talents and abilities. I am eternally grateful and have faith in you!

This book is dedicated to Joanna, for being faith-filled enough to live out her dream.

To all the courageous souls, dedicated to living a life of purpose. I have *faith* in you!

Introduction:

"The unexamined life is not worth living." Socrates

Are you seeking to change your life and live in amazing, purpose-filled ways? Start by asking these two powerful questions:

"Who am I?" and "What am I here for?"

This book asks an individual to examine who they are, as a powerful spiritual being who chose this life and this journey, as a means of growth and exploration. This growth and exploration includes our life stories. Each of us has a life story, a journey that has brought us to the present moment. My hope is that sharing my story will inspire others to examine their life from a different viewpoint, a viewpoint that shows how each part of our life and each experience was purposeful and meant to move us toward the very reason we came to this life, toward our divine purpose.

The greatest source of learning is self-investigation. I have not only stepped onto a path in which I can assist others to heal, but, most importantly, I have stepped onto a path that has brought me healing. I have delved deeply into the practices of yoga, reiki, Buddhism and spirituality in general. I have spent my life, as I have come to understand, exploring the depths of struggle and the heights of love. I know by this experience that, if one individual can heal, it is possible for all. All of us have the choice of whether to be victims in life or be victorious. I choose to be victorious. I choose to have faith that all the experiences that I've seen as challenges or setbacks are, in reality, great gifts. They are the gifts of this human existence. To be victorious is to do the earth walk of faith, to be courageous enough to live life in full openness to each experience and learn and grow from them.

I am a mother, a teacher, a leader, a healer, a guide, a wife, a friend, a business owner, a daughter, a sister and so many other roles. But I am also more than all of these roles. I am a divine being, connected to the whole of the universe. I am a powerful, compassionate, loving and beautiful soul. I am a soul who has chosen a path filled with difficulty and trauma, compassion and forgiveness, joy and sorrow, faith and fear, using each experience of life, difficult and amazing, as a means to learn and grow. Now I teach others to do the same.

I have been chosen and decided to write this book as a guide for others, who want to know more about the power within them, the power of faith that is anchored deep within each of our hearts, anchored deep within each of our souls. I have been chosen and decided to write this book as means of healing from my past in the written form, and, through that healing, to help others do the same.

For many years, I have known I would write a book. I know it is an essential part of my path, to transform the experiences of my past in a way to help others reach understanding. I have worked for many years on my path to heal and transform my individual view of the difficulties of my childhood and young-adult life. The time has come to share my experiences, and to share what I have learned. I have dedicated my life to develop as an individual, as a teacher, as a healer, and to discover and live in alignment with divine purpose. All of us have a divine purpose and share the purpose of service.

My intention is to serve by sharing my story and offering the insight and understanding that I have learned and been taught by all the teachers I have been blessed to study with. My hope is that each individual who reads this book will begin to explore and examine his or her life through the lens of faith. My hope is that the seed of faith that is within each individual becomes activated and enlivened. My hope is that a knowing will awaken within each of the hearts and minds of those who read these pages and understand.

> *"If you have faith even as small as a mustard*
> *seed, you can say to the mountain,*
> *'Move from here to there' and it would move.*
> *Nothing would be impossible."*
> *Matthew 17:20*

With Faith,
all things are possible ...

CHAPTER 1:

Uncommon faith

"When you have come to the edge of all the light you know and are about to drop off into the darkness of the unknown, faith knows one of two things will happen. There will be something solid to stand on, or you will be taught to fly." Patrick Overton

Uncommon faith is a faith of action. Uncommon faith is an unbreakable type of faith that has been tested, tried and found to be a true and substantial power to embrace. Uncommon faith is living in alignment with an understanding that there is something to embrace at all times; faith is present at all times. Uncommon faith is the power to take action in times of great challenge - the challenging times when an individual feels like breaking down or giving in to fears and doubts. In these times especially, a level of uncommon faith emerges in order to guide and support an individual through the difficulty, through the challenge. Uncommon faith is relied upon at all times, the good and the bad, the bitter and the sweet. A faith that is sustaining and ever-present. In the challenging times, a relationship with faith develops that is trusted in as a powerful force of guidance and direction. Uncommon faith is a faith of action that goes through a great challenge and comes out on the other side with a breakthrough of understanding. Uncommon faith is the ability to trust in the most doubt-filled times. It is a place that beckons from deep within, an inner voice that guides you to trust and continue moving forward.

Uncommon faith is a faith of action. Uncommon faith is being bold and daring enough to listen to the inner voice of the soul. This voice is filled with love, encouragement and wisdom. Uncommon faith is brave enough to take the next step, whatever that means for you. The ability to take action without tangible proof that all is going to work out in the end is an action empowered by uncommon faith. For an individual to act, they must have confidence in themselves and realize that they can also be confident in the assistance from the unseen divine forces of the universe. Uncommon faith is belief in things that cannot yet be seen.

Uncommon faith is a degree of faith that is developed through spiritual awakening. Each time you wake up to the possibilities contained in the power of faith, your faith increases and deepens on a very intimate level. Uncommon faith is cumulative; it comes from maturity and spiritual progress. Uncommon faith cannot be taken away by anything or anyone. Uncommon faith is a ground you connect to and develop from deep within yourself. It is the foundation you stand on and make decisions from. Uncommon faith grounds you to your knowing and relies on the wisdom of experience. The wisdom of experience is what makes it unshakeable, impeccable, unbreakable, unfathomable and impenetrable. It is radical, it is all-powerful and it can change your life and the view of the life you have had thus far. This is a level of faith that you will not abandon as soon as you think things are not going your way. It is the kind of faith that allows you to remain steadfast in your intentions and steadfast in making your dreams come true. Uncommon faith dares to dream big and dares to do what is necessary to bring that dream to life, to bring it from imagination to reality.

Uncommon faith allows for all things to become possible. It gives you the power to believe in your visions, in your dreams and in your abilities. Uncommon faith is the courage to allow things in your life to move in a dynamic and fluid way. Anchor deeply into this kind of faith and nothing of the world can break it, touch it or take it. Uncommon faith is an active faith. Uncommon faith is activated by the power of your heart to open, to trust, to love and to hope for things that may seem impossible.

Uncommon faith does not eliminate doubts and fears, but it eclipses their power one step at a time, one decision at a time. Uncommon faith opens your eyes to the potential and the possibility of things to come.

Uncommon faith is the muscle within you. Uncommon faith is strengthened and grows in your life when you make a choice to do something new. Uncommon faith is to step out into the unknown and risk opening up, standing in the center of your life and declaring with boldness, "*I am worthy of living a life filled with peace, love and purpose.*"

Uncommon faith has a way of putting things in order for you. When ignited, it burns away your limiting beliefs. Uncommon faith will move you toward the places you need to examine inside yourself and inside your life. When you ignite this level and degree of faith, let go and be willing to step out of comfort and the known. It will take you into uncharted territory. Uncommon faith will propel you toward your vision and purpose. Uncommon faith is the power that can not only change your life, but also affect the entirety of the world. Each person who chooses this kind of faith changes the world in powerful, inspiring and amazing ways. Uncommon faith is a knowing at the level of the soul; it takes you beyond the mind, beyond the stories of your past and beyond current circumstance. Uncommon faith ignites the full potential contained within you for your life.

Uncommon faith is a level of faith that has supernatural powers and is not limited by where you are now and what you believe. It moves you dynamically and fluidly toward what is meant to be and what is possible for you. Uncommon faith encourages you from within and guides you purposefully in your life. Uncommon faith overrides all excuses and all fears and declares, "*Yes, I can. Yes, I will take a bold step toward purpose, a bold step toward healing, and a bold step of faith.*"

Every action you take in uncommon faith brings great reward. Uncommon faith activates divine forces in the universe. Uncommon faith trusts in that which cannot be seen but knows to be true and possible. Develop this type

With faith all things are possible. ○○

of faith and allow for the uncommon blessings that come with uncommon faith. Uncommon faith would be easy if we had a guarantee.

Uncommon faith comes from a place that sees the whole picture of your life, where you are and where you are meant to go. Uncommon faith sees who you believe you are and then gently guides you to discover who you truly are. Uncommon faith does not need a guarantee; it does not concern itself with such things. Uncommon faith is a power that encourages you to surrender your fears, your doubts and your disbelief. Uncommon faith is accepting and relying upon the great and divine power inside of you. Faith is the basis of all good things. From faith springs trust, hope and peace, just to name a few. Uncommon faith takes dedication and work; it is a muscle strengthened through action. Uncommon faith engages your divine will. It is declaring boldly, in faith, *"I will succeed, I will prosper, I will be happy, and I will live a life of purpose."*

Uncommon faith transforms the stumbling blocks of the past into stepping-stones leading an individual to future heights. When these stumbling blocks are transformed through wisdom and understanding, they no longer hinder you. They are understood as the foundation of wisdom and learning. Uncommon faith transforms the perception of the trials of life. Through the eyes of faith, the adversities you may have experienced are seen as means of learning about:

- compassion
- strength
- courage
- dedication
- honor
- resilience
- love
- forgiveness

You experience the transformative power of faith every time you take a step into the unknown and move in ways you never thought possible. Uncommon faith is the strength to leave an unhealthy situation, the dedication to your dream that accepts the promotion that moves you across the country. Uncommon faith means to honor who you are, to never accept less than what you deserve, to love and dare to be loved, and to have compassion to transform the view of the past and heal through forgiveness. Uncommon faith trusts enough to open the heart in order to release anger, doubt and pain. Uncommon faith is stronger than any fear or doubt. Uncommon faith is well worth your efforts to grow and strengthen.

When you shake a bottle of soda, pressure builds, it wants to explode, it needs to. This is the way I would describe Joanna. She walked into my office with a baseball cap on, her head down, obviously in pain. She had the energy of someone I would describe as defeated. Joanna was referred to me by a friend; she was at the end of her rope and decided what did she have to lose? This is often the place in which I end up working with people. The work I do is less tangible than a prescription of anti-depressants. The work I do is less about a diagnosis and more about discovery. The work I do requires a level of faith, trust and dedication. It asks an individual to look a little deeper and explore things from the inside out.

Joanna had been diagnosed with an auto-immune disorder, but the cause of this disorder was unclear. She would come in broken out in hives, depressed, confused and defeated. Joanna told me her passion was singing. She knew it was her God-given ability and felt like it was her purpose in life. She knew it with conviction, yet she was not living in alignment with her purpose. She explained that at one time she had a record deal, and yet this record was never released to the public. This experience left her questioning her purpose. She had resigned to the fact that maybe she wasn't meant to share her voice in the world in a big way. She was doing her best to live ordinary life, and settle for less than living on purpose.

In truth, Joanna's spirit cannot be held down or held back. She has a presence bigger than a skyscraper, her voice carries for miles and her laugh is infectious. I had faith that she was meant to share her gifts with the world. I had faith that this could be the cause of her poor health and depression. We explored this concept deeply in our work together. Each time we met, Joanna opened up to another level of exploration, a level that says something inside is not in alignment and what you are seeing on the outside is an indicator of that misalignment ~ that essentially, the autoimmune disorder, depression and difficul ties came from living out of alignment with her purpose. She is meant to sing. She is an entertainer. She is meant to share her gifts and abilities with the world.

Joanna faithfully did her work to forgive, heal and find her voice again. She came to the understanding that settling for anything other than living on purpose was no longer acceptable. She wanted to, needed to, explode. She was that proverbial soda bottle, ready to burst. With that, she opened her heart for a new beginning. With faith, she opened herself to new opportunities. When she did that, opportunity came knocking. She now is back out on the road, touring, singing and living out her dreams. With faith, her dreams are coming to life in new and expanded ways.

UNCOMMON FAITH

Faith-filled Testimonial

"I believe God puts people in our lives at just the right time and for just the right purpose. He certainly sent me an angel in Felicia. I have been a performer my whole life. My journey has had many highs and many lows. I was accepted to Juilliard at age 16. Then the road led me to Nashville where I started performing around town and eventually got a publishing deal and a record deal. I worked diligently to make the best record I could make, yet the record never got released. The disappointments I have faced have affected every area of my life, including my health. There were many times I wanted to give up, but as I searched my heart, I knew I was not to quit singing.

When I met Felicia, I had been diagnosed with an auto-immune disease and there was not a doctor anywhere that could tell me the cause or the cure of my problem. I was completely at the end of my rope and was open to try anything at the point. A friend suggested Felicia, and we started working together with reiki. Her intuition confirmed many things in my life that I had questions about and her amazing energy and healing work slowly started taking effect. I remember one day I walked into her studio all broken out in hives, and when we were done with the session that day the hives were completely gone. That told me the emotional healing work was the right path for me. Sometimes it's hard to face your own truths, but Felicia's approach and delivery of things you need to hear is gentle when needed, yet she stands firm in making sure you don't miss the point!

At the time I met Felicia, my self-esteem and faith level was nearly depleted. I was looking at a complete change in my life, which possibly involved laying down my dream of music and getting on what I felt would be an easier way of life by just getting a job, working my 9-to-5 day and going

With faith all things are possible. ⃝

home and just being OK with that. She quickly confirmed that if I chose that path I would lose all happiness, prosperity and peace in my life because my life involves music and it always will. That path meant I was choosing to live small instead of stepping up to all God had for me. She worked with me to build my faith and confidence back up, and by the time we got done, the symptoms of my auto-immune disease were gone. I was off all of my medication, which was a complete miracle. I felt better than I had in years. I felt myself slowly coming back to life. I still had not seen the next door open for me with my music, but I felt like something good was going to happen. That is what faith is all about: standing in the gap between what has been your truth and the next truth in your life to come. It's a very hard place to stand and believe, but it truly is our cycle of life.

Shortly thereafter, I was asked to join one of the biggest country music tours of the year. I still had my fears because I knew my health was so fragile and I knew I needed to be strong to withstand the grueling schedule and toll on my body this tour would bring. It was then that I turned back to Felicia to help me through those fears and once again confirm that I was on the right path. I have now started the tour and my faith guides me to know that from this opportunity bigger and better opportunities will come.

Stay your course. Your heart will lead you to your truth, but I believe God allows people to come into our lives to confirm the things He is saying to you. Felicia has been on an incredible journey herself and has taken all of the things in her life both good and bad and purposefully turned them toward helping to heal others. Her gift is unique and amazing and I know this book will bless anyone that reads it. Stay strong and keep the faith!"

Joanna Cotten

Step out of all you have known and experience faith going to work in your life.

Apply the Lesson
GETTING IN TOUCH WITH FAITH

Meditation:

Find yourself in a comfortable environment, some-where with minimum distractions so that you can be undisturbed for a period of time. Sit comfortably either on the floor or in a chair. If you are seated on the floor, have blankets or pillows under your bottom for support. If you are seated in a chair, either gather the legs under you or have the feet firmly planted upon the ground.

Sit with the spine straight, attentive to your posture. Place your hands lightly on your lap, palms facing either up or down. Let your eyes softly close and take a few moments to become quiet and attentive to the breath. Thoughts will come and thoughts will go; become undis-turbed by thoughts by remaining attentive to the breath.

Bring your awareness to rest on the center of the chest, the spiritual heart, feeling the breath flow in and out, the chest rising up and down as each breath flows in and out.

When you are ready, begin:

On your next inhale, quietly inside state: "I have"

On your next exhale, quietly inside state: "faith."

Each cycle of breath affirms your faith. Simply repeat, in rhythm with the breath.

Inhale, quietly inside state: "I have"

Exhale, quietly inside state: "faith."

"I have faith. I have faith."

Continue in this manner for up to 5 to 10 minutes

Now, in this quiet space contemplate these two questions:

What does faith mean to me?

What do I have faith in about myself?

With faith all things are possible.

When you are ready, take a deep breath and gently allow your eyes to open. Take out your journal and write down your responses:

🌼 What does faith mean to me?

🌼 What do I have faith in about myself?

Example:

🌼 I have faith in my ability to

_____.

🌼 I have faith in the

_____ of my heart.

Let each moment of your day, each step you take be in the consciousness of faith.

Inhale: "I have"

Exhale: "faith."

I have faith. I have faith.

That's a good start. Now let's explore this deeper.

CHAPTER 2

Faith is essential

"Be bold and mighty forces will come to your aid." Basil King

The times when individuals are at their lowest and feel like giving up and giving in to fear, doubts, anger, worries or overwhelming grief are when faith is essential and necessary. Uncommon faith is known and understood as the place to hold onto. Faith is essential and necessary because it is the light that leads you out of those low places. It shines from within, guiding you toward what is above you. It guides you toward understanding and freedom. It takes faith to know there is another way to be, another option. Uncommon faith knows, without a doubt, that you are not meant to stay in the low places. Uncommon faith is the light breaking through the darkness. Uncommon faith is the wisdom of knowing where you are is not where you are meant to stay.

In my path, if I had known how important faith was and understood it to be a part of me, I might not have stumbled so many times or so hard. These were the places in life when I went against the guidance and settled for less than what I deserved. The power of faith in my life on a conscious level has allowed me to move forward in amazing ways without stumbling. I am a testament to this power. I have been able to transform my past into my purpose. When I follow this divine guidance, it leads me toward heights of success and never lets me down. It always leads me in the right direction, the direction that brings learning and growth. I have learned to trust in the guidance that comes from within me, whether I call it instinct, a gut feeling, intuition or faith. I have learned to trust the guidance that encourages movement forward. My faith empowers me to make difficult changes. I have learned to trust and have faith in myself.

I have discovered that within the breakdown is the place where the voice of faith can be heard. It is the place where an individual has exhausted one's self physically and mentally and is at a point where they will allow the voice of faith to emerge. They will finally begin to tune in and listen. It is the place where an individual admits they just don't know anymore and, finally, and sometimes literally, lie flat on their back, look up and ask for assistance: *Show me, help me.* This is a supreme act of faith. Uncommon faith turns to things that cannot be seen and becomes open to assistance. The problem is that an individual just doesn't understand or know where each experience is taking them, what it is showing them, and how to relate to things differently. Uncommon faith will keep the heart open to assistance, to learning and to growth. Uncommon faith teaches an individual how to relate to one's self and life in a way that heals and releases struggle and pain.

Faith isn't only there for the tough situations, the larger dramas in our lives; sometimes the most colorful declaration of faith comes to us during our regular day to day lives, tucked in between the mundane and the even less spectacular.

It was a typical day for me, full of getting the kids' lunches ready for camp, seeing my regular set of three or four clients at my healing practice, teaching yoga, doing laundry and tying up loose ends on projects for my website. Like most days, I was moving from experience to experience, but that day I was falling behind, not quite on task. I started feeling uneasy and thinking "I can't do all of this."

"I can't do this" is a common mantra from my childhood when the chores and responsibilities overwhelmed me. "I can't do all this." I picked up the kids in a typical fashion, except I was late. "I can't do all of this." I watched my children pile

FAITH IS ESSENTIAL

into the car from the rearview mirror and both their eyes and words were reinforcing the fact that, "No, I cannot do this. I am a failure. I am failing them. I am failing my job, my work and my clients. I can't do all of this." In that moment, overwhelming feelings arose from deep inside me, and I found myself crying in the car on the way home. By the time I reached the house, I was sobbing. And then, the pain, my old enemy, returned to my neck with each spasm, and I wasn't sure what to do. A fear rose inside of me that I would be unable to meet all the demands of my life, that I could not do everything. The sobbing contained my fear, doubt, anger, frustration and sadness.

"I can't do all of this."

We got home. I immediately went downstairs to my office, my sanctuary. This is where I am safe. This is where I can fall apart. And I did. Tears streamed down my face, my breath uneasy with each sob. The pain in my neck increased. "I can't do of all this. I can't do this." I cried and cried and cried. I cried out to God, the Angels, to anyone who would listen. I called out, "I don't know if I can do all of this; I don't know if I'm enough."

"Have faith, Felicia. Have faith," is what I heard. The voice was not uncommon; in fact, it seemed similar to my own, but I couldn't quite trust it.

Faith? In what? Faith that I can do this? Faith that I can handle all that is on my plate?

And then the internal dialogue between fear and faith began. With each mention of faith, my fearful mind retorted back in doubt. What do you mean by faith? The battle continued -- because even a small moment in our lives can spark a battle -- until I heard, "Have faith in you."

A warmth resided over me like a blanket to keep me safe and secure. I stopped sobbing and was guided to my bookshelf, where I randomly chose a book, but there are no random coincidences on our paths. Everything is purposeful, just as the message that day was purposeful. The book I reached for contained the story of Joshua·

With faith all things are possible. ᏩᎤ

23

*"When Joshua spoke to the Lord in the
day when the Lord delivered up the
Amorites before the children of Israel,
and he said in the sight of Israel:*

*Sun, stand still over Gibeon; and
Moon, in the Valley of Aijalon.*

*So the sun stood still, and the moon stopped,
till the people defeated their enemies.*

*So the sun stood still in the midst
of heaven, and did not hastened to
go down for about a whole day.*

*And there has been no day like
that, before it or after it,*

*that the Lord heeded a voice of a
man; for the Lord fought for Israel."*

Joshua 10:12-14

In the story, Joshua is in battle with his enemy. He is running out of daylight, and he knows that if the sun goes down on
this day he will be unable to defeat the enemy and he will have
to rise again for more battles. So he had uncommon faith. He
was bold and he asked, "Stop the sun in the sky, so I can have
more daylight and complete my task."

His kind of uncommon faith was heard in the world of
heaven. The sun stopped in the sky. Joshua was able to defeat
the enemy that day, because he was so bold to ask, and bold
enough to have uncommon faith, because with faith all things
are possible. There had never been a day like that before and
has not been one since. The Bible says that the sun stood still
that day until Joshua won the battle. The story shows the power
of uncommon faith – a level of faith so strong, so bold and so
courageous that the sun stopped in the sky.

The interesting thing about breakdowns is that they are
really breakthroughs. As I read the story of Joshua, I saw that
faith was leading me to a story about the courageous man, this
amazing warrior, who knew he needed help and had enough

FAITH IS ESSENTIAL

faith to ask for it. He had enough faith to know that even though this was quite a hefty request, God would indeed stop the sun so Joshua could defeat his enemies. Could I have the same bold declaration in faith? Yes.

The day of my breakdown was transformed with this story. With faith, I asked for guidance and received it. With faith, I asked for help and received it. With faith, I rose that day and had the courage to make some changes in my life. That day, faith did not steer me in the direction of being able to complete all my tasks. It did not show me that I could, because I already knew I could. Instead, I was presented with the thought, "Do I need to?"

After that moment on that typical day, I started reevaluating want I needed to accomplish. I had decisions to make. I was being pulled in new directions. I tuned into my internal GPS, my internal guidance. Seeing that I needed a little time to myself, I took a vacation to visit one of my teachers. That night, I dreamt of a woman who writes and assists people in writing books. That night, faith intervened in my dreams, showing me that this is this book I needed to write. Other projects fell away as faith guided me to let go and instructed me that as long as I stay true to my life's purpose, I can choose my path to it, without fear, because I am walking in faith. The statement "Have faith" has served me numerous times on this journey and in the completion of this book, and it all arose from a typical day of a working mother. In the midst of daily life, my breakdown was an opportunity for growth, and the next step on my path was revealed.

In order to be helped, an individual must be bold enough to ask for the assistance they need. The amount an individual will ask for is often based on the limits they place upon themselves. Having faith first and foremost in yourself is of monumental importance on the path. Having faith in yourself is the first step to activating the faith needed to ask for things like stopping the sun in the sky! Develop faith first in yourself and your ability to act. This ignites a new energy in your life. Faith opens you up to the fact that where you are is not the end; it can be the beginning. Any time you open up and allow for faith to arise from within, a new beginning becomes possible. Uncommon faith has the power to invite and open the door for light ~ the light of hope, the light of compassion, the light of true wisdom and soul-filled understanding. All things are possible in the energy of faith. Uncommon faith teaches you to trust in the invisible and divine powers alive in the universe.

A circumstance will occur in your life as a means of moving you toward living in alignment with divine purpose. A circumstance will arise to move you toward the next thing. It is the push of life, but it is also the pull of destiny, the pull of divine purpose. The day of my breakdown saw the simultaneous play of these two forces. The breakdown was the push of life; it brought the problem to the surface. The breakdown was also the pull of destiny; it was time to take action and write this book. My faith transformed this experience into an opportunity for growth and healing.

When you act with uncommon faith and move, the circumstance will change. I acted in uncommon faith by letting go of projects and starting something new, something I had never done before. When I acted in faith, the doors of opportunities opened all around me. I was guided to a program that gave me a format to begin this book; I have been connected to the resources and the right people in order to make it all happen. Uncommon faith is carrying you to destiny and divine purpose, it moves dynamically and fluidly. When you remain stuck in fear and are unable to take action, the circumstance continues and the struggle continues. When I took a bold step of faith, my struggles subsided.

> *"F-E-A-R has two meanings: 'Forget*
> *Everything And Run' or 'Face Everything*
> *And Rise.' The choice is yours."* **Zig Ziglar**

The earth walk of faith is the choice to face everything and rise. Meet the challenges of life in the energy of faith. The earth walk of faith is bold enough, courageous enough to step out of the safe zone, the comfort zones, and into the faith zone. Uncommon faith will take you into uncharted territory. Uncommon faith is walking on the earth, living your life in a new way. Uncommon faith is the power to choose faith over fear. Uncommon faith expands your life in amazing and unimaginable ways. The earth walk of faith is living in alignment with the answer to the question, "What am I here for?"

Melissa bubbles with love. She has a heart as pure as gold. When I met her, she was at a place that I describe as the edge of all that is known, the place that can be described as hitting a wall. Melissa had hit her wall and was caught there. She was caught up in her doubts and fears, and unable to take a next step. She knew the life she was experiencing when I met her was not the life she was meant to live. She was seeking the answer to the question, "What am I here for?" She knew that it was time to change something, that she desperately needed to make some changes. Without faith in herself and her abilities, she was stuck in doubt and fear. In order to make changes and live a life on purpose, faith is the essential and necessary component that the individuals I work with need to reconnect to. Reconnect versus create faith. Faith is ever-present; it is there right behind the doubt and fear.

In our work together, I guided her to go deeper and connect to the voice of faith in a clear and powerful way. She needed to listen to the voice of faith inside and tune into the message it was broadcasting. She had to change the station; tune into the station that was broadcasting words of faith, courage and hope. This voice was encouraging her and guiding her in new ways and toward new things. Although Melissa was experiencing anxiety and confusion, she also knew this was not what was meant for her. Melissa's dedication to healing is inspiring. She exudes love and courage as she step by step, moment by moment follows her voice of faith to her divine purpose. She lives in alignment with her divine purpose, which I know is about love, sharing love and loving others in a way that transforms them. Melissa is a blessing to this world and all those that have the privilege of knowing her.

With faith all things are possible. ᏽ

Faith-filled testimonial

"When I first met Felicia, I was facing a big decision, struggling with anxiety and, although I didn't realize it at the time, I had lost faith and confidence in myself. A trusted friend referred me to her. I had no idea what to expect from our session, but I knew I needed help. That session began my healing journey. Working with Felicia over the years has allowed me to find my voice again and trust my intuition. It hasn't always been easy, but I have felt love, support and guidance every step of the way. This transformation continues to impact every aspect of my life in a positive way. And though I still don't have all the answers, I have faith that my internal compass is guiding me along the path of my purpose. And for that and so much more, I will always be grateful."

Melissa W.

Having faith in your yourself is the first step to activating the faith needed to ask for, and to be bold enough to ask for things, like stopping the sun in the sky!

⟨⟩ Apply the Lesson
GETTING IN TOUCH WITH
WHAT AM I HERE FOR

Meditation:

Find yourself in a comfortable environment, some-where with minimum distractions so that you can be undisturbed for a period of time. Sit comfortably either on the floor or in a chair. If you are seated on the floor, have blankets or pillows under your bottom for support. If you are seated in a chair, either gather the legs under you or have the feet firmly planted upon the ground.

Sit with the spine straight, attentive to your posture. Place your hands lightly on your lap, either palms fac-ing up or down. Let your eyes softly close and take a few moments to become quiet and attentive to the breath. Thoughts will come and thoughts will go; remain undis-turbed by thoughts by staying attentive to the breath.

Continue in this manner for 5 to 10 minutes.

Bring your attention to rest on the forehead, the space between the physical eyes, the energy center of creative vi-sion. Allow your internal gaze to be as if you were looking up gently between the eyes. Breathe and gently focus your attention on that internal gaze.

As your attention rests in this space, freely contemplate:
Without limitation of time, money or current circumstance:

    ✸ What do I want to create in my life?

    ✸ What is the dream that I want to see turn into reality?

    ✸ What is the vision for my future?

Continue in this manner for up to 5 to 10 minutes, simply contemplating these three questions.

With faith all things are possible. ⟨⟩

When you are ready, take a deep breath and gently allow your eyes to open. Take out your journal and write down your responses:

⚬ What do I want to create in my life?

⚬ What is the dream that I want to see turn into reality?

⚬ What is the vision for my future?

Time to think big! Uncommon faith dares to dream big! Think at the level of Joshua, the level of daring, bold uncommon faith; faith so powerful the sun stops in the sky. Declare what you want and need for your life. Write freely.

⚬ What is my bold declaration of faith?

CHAPTER 3

Faith is within you

"You cannot heal what you cannot feel." Felicia McQuaid

My first memories of growing up are of living in New York City with my mother Louanna, father Felix and brother Jeff, living in an apartment, spending time with the neighbors (who took care of us while my mother did the shopping), and playing in the courtyard.

Felix went from nothing, born in a small village in Puerto Rico, to someone who could provide for his kids in New York City. His parents never married, and his mother died when he was 2, leaving his grandmother to raise him. Because of poverty, Felix did not have any shoes or many clothes to wear, and stopped attending school after second grade. He worked for his father cleaning roosters for his cockfighting ring. At 12, his grandmother sent him to Ohio to live with an aunt, and then to the Bronx, New York, with an uncle, where he shined shoes and saved enough money to start his life. He grew up as a street kid making his own way, but gambling and hustling would still be part of who he was.

He met my mother in New York. She had left her home in Kansas and gone out into the world to find her way, saving her pennies to vacation in New York. Three days into her trip, the universe brought these two together in New York City. I'm sure my mother was enamored with Dad's street sense and worldly experiences. He worked at the nightclubs and gambled. He made his own way. My mother grew up an only child in a small town in Kansas called Council Grove, which is where I was born. Going to New York was a big step for her. She stepped out of the small, safe life of Kansas, a life of being an only child raised by two loving parents, and made a big decision to move out into the world and find her way. I remember her speaking of the first *few years of being with Dad as good times, times when they got along, they were in love, and things were good and new. They met in June 1969, married three months later, and I was born in 1972. My mother came home from New York to have me in her hometown of Council Grove. She wanted to have her mother, Helen, present for the birth. My father, Felix, who I'm named after, stayed behind in New York.*

I know that I was truly loved when I came into the world. I also know that during that time there was difficulty, and I have memories of being in the crib and hearing the fights and screams that eventually escalated to abuse between my parents. My father became a worse and worse alcoholic, a more dedicated gambler and an angrier individual as the years went on. He had two personalities: When he was good, he was oh-so-good and loving, but his Mr. Hyde side was cruel. He would pull my mother by the hair and push her around, waking me with their fights. My brother was born two years after me, and I think the strain of a second child worsened the mood in our home. My father was the type of man who liked to have focus upon him. As my mother's focus turned to the children, he became angrier. I believe he loved us, but I also believe his anger, addictions and frustrations won him over.

A Tale of Two Wolves:
An elderly Cherokee told his Grandson about a battle that goes on inside people.

He said, "My son, the battle is between two wolves inside us all.

One is black. It is anger, envy, jealousy, sorrow, regret, greed, arrogance, self-pity, guilt, resentment, lies, pride, superiority and ego.

The other is white. It is joy, peace, love, hope, serenity, humility, kindness, empathy, generosity, truth, compassion and faith."

The Grandson thought for a moment, and then asked, "Which wolf wins?"

The old Cherokee simply replied, "The one that you feed."

FAITH IS WITHIN YOU

When I think about my father, I recall encountering the black and white wolves that existed inside of him. I was his firstborn and I recall my mother speaking about him buying me beautiful dresses, the best of the best. I was named after him; my name, Felicia, means "happiness." When I learned the meaning of my name, I wondered if my name was a prophecy of the life I was meant to live. When someone is happy, it means they are living in the light, living on purpose. Happiness is easy when you are living a life of purpose. When you know who you are and what you are meant to do, it brings happiness. Happiness is not about what we have or don't have. Happiness is about knowing who you are and the ability to live on purpose, and to feel purposeful in life. My father had a hard time with happiness. More often he chose to feed the black wolf, the one filled with anger, resentment, pride and lies.

My father used to frequent the horse racetracks, something he and my mother would do before kids came into the picture, and at times he would take all of us along. I was around 18 months old on this particular day at the races; I even have a picture of me that was placed in the New York Post.

I am sitting happily on a bench, tiny legs dangling, eating a giant hot dog. This little girl with short blonde curls looks like she has everything – front page of a well-known newspaper, two loving parents who spoil her with hot dogs, and a glorious city as her backdrop. It's just another day at the races, another fun-filled family outing in New York City, a day for us to spend time with my father doing what he enjoyed – betting on horses and having a few drinks. Behind the fading black ink of my news-printed angelic face is the true story.

The day started off fun, but as it progressed Felix lost more bets, causing him to drink more (and vice versa), resulting in money lost. Possibly my mother egged him on, angry at the money wasted that could have been used for groceries. Maybe she looked at him a certain way and his guilt about the money set him off, or maybe it was the whiskey on his breath that pushed him over the edge, but the abuse that had remained behind closed doors was shoved into the open. In the parking lot of the racetrack, Felix yelled at my mother and smacked her jaw so fiercely that it went through her skin. He punched her so hard that, to this day, she has trouble with her jaw. My mother had to go with me in tow to clean her face at the nearest restroom. This was not during a time when strangers intervened and helped. No one came to my mother's side or called the police, and after she gathered herself together, we got into the car with Felix, and he took us home.

For a long time, I did not allow myself to remember these things. They were too painful to be real, but when you heal and desire healing, the doors inside of you open, so you can truly see the path that has brought you to where you are. To transform pain, you must first acknowledge it. You cannot heal what you cannot feel.

This is just one of the memories that have come forward to me. There are other memories of him coming home late at night, intoxicated, angry, having lost money, and taking it out on my mother. He would yell and pull her around our small apartment by her hair, with me watching all of it. I would do my best to spend time with my brother and keep him safe and keep him out of the violence that was happening around us. My mother would do her best to hide her bruises and spend time with us when he was away, but how do you ever really forget, especially when it is an ongoing experience? So even when he wasn't there, his anger and the abuse was still there with us.

My mother would say to me that she thought I had a bubble of light around me, which my father could never penetrate. She told me that he would never turn his anger on me and that when he would see me, it would disarm him. Many times he would stop fighting and abusing her if I stood in his way. It would break the cycle, even if just for moment. When I reflect on my father, I real-ize that he must've been in an enormous amount of pain to be able to hurt people, especially the ones he loved. I also realize that my light, the happiness and love that I brought into his life, was powerful. It was powerful enough that it would remind him of love and pull him away from his pain. When he could pull away from his pain, he could stop inflicting pain on others.

As a child, I was always very aware of what was going on around me. I remember always standing back and observing oth-ers and feeling things very deeply. I have learned through my pro-

FAITH IS WITHIN YOU

cess of healing and transforming these difficulties that these are the very qualities that make me so strong and powerful! I have a great ability to stand back, a great ability to witness difficulty, and a great ability to feel things so strongly. For a long time, I thought these abilities were a curse. It made things very difficult when I was surrounded by only anger and pain. With faith, I know that within me is a power stronger than anger and pain. This force is inside us all, but we must learn to utilize it. Faith transforms the way you see things. Faith transforms your understanding of things. In this kind of transformative understanding, the things you have thought of as a curse or challenge are now known to be a great gift.

I asked my mother what made her leave, what gave her the courage to admit the abuse to her parents, and what gave her the courage to leave my father. She told me it was me, that at 4 years old, I picked up the phone and called my grandmother, my hero, Helen Heaton. I told her that we needed to come to live with her. I insisted that she send us money, so we could go to Kansas and leave my father.

In a healing session, I recalled the memory that was the catalyst for this call. I was 4 years old. My father kept my mother on a fairly short leash. He liked her to be home whenever he returned from work or one of his drinking binges. Saturday was the day she was allowed to shop, since he would be working at the bar. My mother used to leave us with a neighbor while my father was working and she was out. She dropped us off that morning; she usually spent her one day of freedom shopping and picked us up in the evening. This Saturday, however, my father came home early and picked us up from the neighbor's apartment instead; our neighbor was hesitant to let us go with him, for it was the middle of the day, and already his eyes were glazed over and his gait sluggish.

But what was she to do? This was a different time when people kept to their own business and, after all, he was our father. We walked through the door of our apartment, and his nasty disposition wafted into our home like the whiskey on his breath. He was livid, charging down the halls, cussing, and wanting to wail on someone. That someone most likely was my mother, but she was gone. When a person has that much anger building inside, he or she will feel the need to release it. The closest body to unleash his wrath on was my 2-year-old brother. Felix backed him into a corner. My brother began to cry. This set my father off even more, triggering a slew of verbal abuses attacking my brother's manhood. As I stared into the rage piercing through Felix's eyes, I knew that he would kill my brother. I stood between them, like the many times before, but this time stone-cold with fear. Without hesitation, as if a knee-jerk response, Felix smacked me with full force, and I flew across the room. Everything stopped. Time stood still. Felix, too, seemed shocked, and it was over. He left.

When my mother came home that day, she and the neighbor who watched us found my brother and me alone in the apartment. She could tell that I had been crying. I told her the whole ordeal with my brother and how my father had yelled and hit him, but I hid the abuse I had endured. It's what I was taught to do. I hid it from myself for over 30 years. That day affected me deeply and left a deep trauma within me, within my consciousness. That day I lost faith in myself as being special.

Until then, no matter how angry my father got, how drunk he was, how abusive he was with everyone else, he had never turned that abuse upon me. I was special. I would stand in front of him and scream for him to stop when the abuse reached escalating points. I was special. I would stand in front of him and prevent him from hurting my brother. I was special. I could stand in front of him, and he would stop. He would not harm me. I was special. That day changed things. I lost the light inside me and the knowledge that I was special. I was changed in that moment. In the healing process and the transformation of the pain of that day, I've realized that my journey has been to get back to knowing that girl with golden hair and skin who emanates pure light, back to knowing that I am special.

To make the choice at 4 years old to hold that experience inside was a conscious choice on some level. I wanted to help my mother, so I chose to hide my shame, to hide my pain. This experience was planted so deep inside of me that it took more than 30 years to come to the surface. It was shortly after that day that I encouraged, insisted and possibly demanded that my mother let me speak to my grandmother.

FAITH IS WITHIN YOU

My grandmother wired us money. We snuck away at night on a bus when my father was away. We took hardly any of our possessions. Only the neighbor who watched us knew we were leaving. We had to get back to Kansas, where we were safe and out of his reach. We made it to Kansas before he realized it and stopped us.

I realize that my mom was being held prisoner by him, her spirit so broken down that she couldn't leave on her own. I have faith that my father's abuse turned on me was the only way we would have ever left. It was the circumstance that got us all out of harm's way. For a long time, I carried a lot of guilt about leaving. I carried a lot of guilt because of all the things that happened from that point on in my life and in my family. I wondered if things would've been different. I wondered if my father would have transformed in some way. I wondered if my parents could have figured out how to make things work, and if we could have been a happy family. In the light of faith, truth is revealed. I have come to realize that in that moment I was serving a divine purpose. I know deep within my heart that the abuse would have continued, not only for my mother and my brother, but also for me.

I have faith that my divine purpose showed itself there, to save my family. At that age, I had no understanding of faith or guidance. But from somewhere innately within me, the guidance was so strong that it moved my whole family out of that situation. Faith saved our lives in many ways, ways I understand and ways I may never understand.

Having faith enough to get in touch with how you feel is the power needed in order to heal.

❧ *Apply the Lesson*

GETTING IN TOUCH WITH HOW YOU FEEL

Meditation:

Find yourself in a comfortable environment. Somewhere with minimum distractions and that you can be undisturbed for a period of time. Lie down comfortably with support under your knees and under your head. Place your hands alongside the body with your palms facing up. Let your eyes softly close and take a few moments to become quiet and attentive to the breath. Thoughts will come and thoughts will go. Simply remain attentive to the breath.

Gently bring your attention to your body, your whole body, simply breathing and feeling your body rest along the support underneath it. Simply breathing in and simply breathing out.

Continue in this manner for up to 5 to 10 minutes.

As your attention rests on your body,
Contemplate: What is here now?

* Simply notice the sensations, feelings, colors, words or thoughts that arise as you contemplate this question.

* Bring your attention to your legs. As your attention rests on the legs, allow them to relax ever more deeply.

* Bring your attention to your belly. As your attention rests on the belly, allow it to relax ever more deeply.

* Bring your attention to your chest. As your attention rests on the chest; allow it to relax ever more deeply.

- Bring your attention to your arms. As your attention rests on the arms, allow them to relax ever more deeply.

- Bring your attention to your neck. As your attention rests on the neck, allow it to relax ever more deeply.

- Bring your attention to your head. As your attention rests on the head, allow it to relax ever more deeply into the support underneath you.

As your attention rests on your body, your whole body, simply:

Contemplate: What is here now?

- Simply notice the sensations, feelings, colors, words or thoughts that arise as you contemplate this question.

- Bring your attention to the center of your chest, placing your hands on your heart, the spiritual heart, the home of faith within you. Feel the flow of breath, feel the flow of the life force moving in and out of you.

As your attention rests on your heart:

Contemplate: What is here now?

- Simply notice the sensations, feelings, colors, words or thoughts that arise as you contemplate this question.

- Getting in touch with how you feel is essential to healing. Healing is part of your divine purpose. You cannot heal what you cannot feel. Faith heals.

When you are ready, take a deep breath and gently allow your eyes to open. Take out your journal:

Explore the question: What is here now?

- What did you notice in the exploration of your body?

- What did you notice in the exploration of your heart?

Throughout your day take time to get in touch with how you feel by simply pausing wherever you are and take a deep breath in and out and contemplate: What is here now?

CHAPTER 4

Faith is insightful

"At the center of your being you have the answer; you know who you are and you know what you want." Lao Tzu

There are moments in our life when the doors of faith open from the inside. When these doors of faith open from the inside, two fundamental and necessary spiritually powerful questions arise: *"Who am I?"* and *"What am I here for?"* The power contained within these two questions is the power of self-examination and divine understanding. These questions invoke moments of divine enlightenment. These moments are like a flash in the dark, or a call to the light.

These questions come from the level of the soul. The soul already knows the answer to these questions. The soul is the part of you that mapped this journey out from the moment of conception. The soul knows all that will be encountered in this journey of life and it knows the "I" being referred to in these questions. The soul maps out the journey to all the experiences, people and circumstances that are meant to strengthen you, strengthen your faith and strengthen your capacity for love and forgiveness. Since the journey is orchestrated by the soul -- the tools and capabilities to meet each experience -- each person and each circumstance is also contained within you. The soul, the true "I am," uses your experiences and *knows* with conviction and faith that these experiences were designed to make you stronger and to lead you to your divine purpose, the reason you are here.

Asking these questions consciously will open the doors of faith for anyone who dares to ask, examine and understand, *"Who am I?"* and *"What am I here for?"* These questions lead you to becoming enlightened about yourself and your life. They bring about the self-examination required to make change and discover the purpose of your life. Enlightenment is the choice to bring light to your life, the light of faith, the light of the soul. Faith leads you to examine yourself and your life in a new way. These questions lead you toward your true self and your true life purpose. These questions flip the light switch on. Make a conscious choice to turn on the light in the dark. There is no need to stumble and struggle in darkness. Within you are the answers; within you is the light, the map leading you to your true purpose. All you have to do is turn on the light.

> *"No problem can be solved from the same level of consciousness that created it."* **Albert Einstein**

If you want to find a new way, want to feel better, want to know peace and understanding, it requires a leap of faith. It requires a leap of faith to examine the unknown and unseen aspects of yourself. Uncommon faith is the willingness to dive deeper into this self- examination and explore things from the inside out. When you no longer blame others for your past and present difficulties, you take charge of your life and become empowered. Uncommon faith is empowering. Uncommon faith empowers an individual to stop being a victim of life and become victorious in the mindful and purposeful examination of life.

When different questions are asked, different answers are received. Faith-based thinking is solution-based. Faith-based thinking offers a different perspective on the problem itself: If there is a problem, there must also be a solution. Faith-based thinking knows that answers and direction cannot be found in the dark. Asking "Who am

FAITH IS INSIGHTFUL

I?" and "*What am I here for?*" in a conscious way shifted my viewpoint dramatically. It shifted my view from the outside (looking for someone or something to blame) to looking inside myself to find the answers and release blame. I could not change myself or my life until I empowered myself to explore and understand how I got there. The questions of "*Who am I?*" and "*What am I here for?*" peeled back a layer for me to investigate questions like:

- Do I like who I am?

- Am I happy with who I am?

- Do I truly know who I am and what I stand for?

- What am I doing with my life?

Contemplating the question "*Who am I?*" gave me an option to look beyond what I did not like about myself and understand that these things are not the true me, not in the context of spirituality. Contemplating the question "*What am I here for?*" first guided me to understand and investigate "*Where am I?*" When I investigated this, it allowed me to be responsible for the place I was standing, good or bad, and contemplate if this was where I was meant to be and stay.

The true you, the true "I Am," is the eternal, divine aspect of you. It is the part of you that is unchanging no matter your age, where you live or what you do in life. It is the divine piece of the heavens that is part of each one of us. This "I Am" is the observer, the witness, the one who knows all and sees all. This "I Am" is the one within you that is your voice of faith, the voice of the divine. The true "I Am" is more powerful than you know and more real than you may realize. This is the "I Am" that you want to know intimately; it is the true guiding power of your life. It asks that you stop looking outside yourself for direction and answers. It asks you to look within for the answers you seek.

At the age of 28, my life changed forever when from somewhere deep within came the life-affirming, thought-provoking and eternally transformative questions:

"Who am I?" and "What am I here for?"

I was standing in the middle of the place that I frequented regularly, Howl at the Moon, a dueling piano bar that promised plenty of dancing and booze. This was our regular hangout on weekends, weeknights and whenever I and my friends needed to unwind. This night, just like every other, we ended up at the bar, but unlike every other night, I was a little reserved. I didn't feel like drinking. I ordered a beer, but held it more than drank it. My roommate was on the dance floor, but I had no desire to join her, and instead retreated to the barriers and watched, as if I was watching a film where my friends were the stars. I was outside of it all, witnessing my friends out celebrating the end of a week, celebrating what we thought was our freedom. I was celebrating too, but something was different. In the middle of the lights and loud music, a voice that came from within me asked:

"Who are you?

"What are you doing here?"

Her tone was comparable that of your best friend who is fed up with your decisions, as she looks into your eyes and says, "What the hell are you doing here?"

"What do you mean what am I doing here? I'm always here," I replied in my mind.

"Who are you? What are you doing here?"

She sounded like me, but she did not feel like me. It was as if I was standing beside myself, watching myself do what I'd always done, be with the people that I'd always been with, and yet it felt very unfamiliar. In fact, the best way that I can describe it is that I appeared and stood beside myself. Amid the men and women at the bar toasting with their beers or the groups of girlfriends dancing and declaring how much they love each other, the soul of me — the true person that I am, a lighter version of myself at that time, the person that I have come to know throughout this process — stood right next to me and asked:

"Who are you?"

"What are you doing here?"

At the time, I did not realize the depth of these questions and this experience. The rest of the night was odd at best for me. I tried to ignore it, called myself crazy and attempted to resume my life as I had known it. The truth is that I could not ignore it and my life was changed dramatically that night. After that night, I no longer wanted to go out with the same group of friends. I became very curious about who I was. I made a commitment to yoga and meditation. I made a commitment to myself. I wanted to know why I was here. That night brought me into a conscious state of being. It was no longer acceptable to be in pain, no longer tolerable to live in anger. I wanted to experience happiness and joy. I knew that I had some things to figure out and some big changes in store for me.

Six months prior to that night at Howl at the Moon, I had started attending yoga classes, playing around with the idea of meditation, and starting to realize how unhappy and unfulfilled I was. Many of my friendships at the time became less and less appealing, full of drinking and gossip. Many of the superficial people in my life started to disappear, and my yoga practice became stronger; my schedule now revolved around yoga. My interests changed, and I read more spiritual teachings. All of this led to that moment when a lighter, pain-free Felicia questioned my existence.

I did not realize that stepping onto the path of yoga was the first step in transforming the difficulties of my life. Through yoga I shifted my consciousness -- the way I was viewing myself and my life -- in a way that could remove the pain that was blocking my light. Yoga is the supreme path of self-examination. Practicing yoga connected me to the divine being with my heart, the light of me, the true "I Am." Yoga enlightened me about myself and the condition of my body, mind and spirit. Enlightenment is to bring our light into the world. In depression and pain, I could not bring light into the world, for I had lost sight of it. I was lost in the dark, lost inside myself. Yoga revealed light from the inside out. Yoga connected me to the center of my being, where I know who I am and what I am meant to do.

That night I became insightful and understood the importance of making changes. The only way out of pain was to do things differently. Insight is a flash of openness, a flash of light, a flash of consciousness. It is a moment of awakening, a moment of enlightenment. It is a flash in the dark meant to guide you toward the light, toward the truth. Imagine you have been stumbling around in the dark searching for a way out, searching for answers, and suddenly the light comes on. With the light, you are shown clearly where you are standing, literally and metaphorically. With the light, you can see yourself clearly, maybe for the first time. This insight is referred to by many as their "ah-ha" moment. My "ah-ha" was that I was not what or who I thought I was. In the light, I realized that I was not lost; I was actually standing on a path. This was quite a revelation for me because I felt lost and without direction or purpose. I felt lost in the dark, but once the light was shown, I could take action and find my way out of anger and confusion. In the light of awareness, I could investigate why I felt this way. My "ah-ha" revealed how unhappy and unfulfilled I was.

My "ah-ha," this moment of awareness, was the moment my eyes opened fully to the fact that I did not like myself or my life in its current condition. I was stuck; I was angry; I was carrying a chip on my shoulder so heavy that it was creating immense, undeniable physical pain. I was seeing doctors, specialists, massage therapists and chiropractors, and had no physical diagnosis as to why this pain existed. I was prescribed painkillers, muscle relaxers and anti-depressants, none of which alleviated the pain.

That pain was the mystery of my past. It weighed so heavily upon my body and mind that it was depressed me on every level. I believed it to be me and identified with this pain and depression as the very essence of who I was. This moment of awareness opened me up and revealed a different me, a person I did not know how to identify with. The true "I Am" was not angry, it was not in pain, and it was guiding me toward purpose, it was guiding me to heal. Being absent of pain was foreign to me. I could not identify with that experience. My daily experience and consciousness were of heartache and pain. The only voice I was truly listening to was the voice of pain. My body was demanding my attention. It demanded that I step inside, to turn on the light inside of this house, see what was going on, and make some changes. It was the only way to end the pain. It was the only way to end the depression. Enlightenment is essentially learning to stand in the light of who you are. In the light of the soul, you realize what you are meant to be doing with your life and in your life. When you wake up, you realize you are not alone and everything you need is at your disposal. There is light in the dark, and this light is the very sustenance of life.

Every individual receives guidance, but not all recognize it as such. When you begin to ask the real questions of life, *"Who am I?"* and *"What am I here for?,"* the doors of faith swing open inside of you. Many times, faith shows you who you are and what you are meant to be doing by first showing you what you are not and what you need to leave behind. When the voice of the true "I Am" speaks, it guides you to unlock the mystery of you, at the level of being, as human beings, not human doings. The true "I Am" is the being at the center of you.

Awareness is the first step to change and healing; it empowers you. Awareness is the doorway to the present moment. First you have to know where you are and be willing to stand in the light. Light reveals all without discrimination of good or bad. Be aware of the importance of the examination of these two fundamental questions, as they will open the door to the change and healing that needs to take place. To understand who you truly are is to understand that you are not your wounds or your past, but something far greater. These wounds, and the past, are meant to teach things that lead to your true divine purpose, your destiny!

In order to change and stand fully in the power of the true self, shift your consciousness. Instead of investigating where you feel limited, open yourself up for growth. Give yourself permission to stop leaving your dreams and visions in the realm of dreams and the impossible. Set the basis for what is possible in faith.

Dear, sweet, beautiful Emme walked into my clinic full of potential. She had faith that it was time to take a leap. Everything in her life was pushing her, encouraging her, and in some sense, demanding that she do so. She knew she had important things to do and important things to share. Something was holding her back from taking this leap of faith. Her fears and doubts were holding her back. She was giving them power and not even realizing it. The fears and doubts followed her from her past and now stood in front of her as the obstacle to her future.

She had decisions to make, action to take. Uncommon faith is the ability to take action in spite of doubts and fears. This is what Emme was ready to do. Bit by bit, she let go of the past and what no longer served her. She was ready to start a new vocation and live in alignment with her divine purpose. She did this by getting in touch with the true "I Am," the voice of faith. This voice was guiding her to the next step on her path and all she had to do was faithfully follow it. When she did that, I witnessed the power of faith going to work in her life.

FAITH IS INSIGHTFUL

Faith-filled testimonial

"I began working with Felicia at a pivotal point in my life. At that time, I was deeply unfulfilled because I was too scared to express my authentic self, to share my true gifts and passions. Over time, with Felicia's help, I began to do the work of gently peeling back the layers of old wounds and surrendering everything that no longer served me. Bit by bit, healing and forgiveness was made possible and a consciousness grew within me.

I have come to see the truth of my divine light and of the divine support and guidance that is always and abundantly around each and every one of us, if we will only allow ourselves to receive it. I began to trust and have faith in what my inner voice was whispering and guiding me to do. With Felicia's guidance, support and encouragement, I was able to jump off the cliff, fly toward my dreams and create the life I had kept silent in me for so long. I have never been happier because, each and every day, I am living a deeply authentic and fulfilling life of my choosing, no longer holding back my light, but allowing it to shine bright, bright, bright."

Emme W.

When you speak, think and act in an expanded way, in an energy of faith, it allows for the things we imagine to come into reality. New energy, new contemplations and new questions bring forth a new possibility. Envision what you want to create, and allow a new energy to flow through you. What you can conceive of, you can achieve. Conceive of a life of happiness, purpose and peace. Trust that with faith all things are possible.

Having faith enough to investigate "Who am I?"
and "Why I am here?" is what empowers you
from the level of the soul. Soul power will guide
you to the answers you seek.

With faith all things are possible.

~ Apply the Lesson
GETTING IN TOUCH WITH WHO AM I

Meditation:

Find yourself in a comfortable environment. Somewhere with minimum distractions and that you can be undisturbed for a period of time. Sit comfortably either on the floor or in chair. If you are seated on the floor, have blankets or pillows under your bottom for support. If you are seated in a chair, either gather the legs under you or have the feet firmly planted upon the ground.

Sit with the spine straight, attentive to your posture. Place your hands lightly on your lap, palms facing up to signify openness. Let your eyes softly close and take a few moments to become quiet and attentive to the breath. Become ever more deeply connected to the breath, observing the natural ebb and flow of the breath, observing the natural rhythm of you and your breath.

Continue in this manner for 5 to 10 minutes.

In this quiet space, contemplate:

"Who am I?" Ask the question but do not answer it with words; feel the answer. Feel the answer in the breath moving in and out of your body. Feel the answer in the dynamic flow of life force energy moving within you. Simply feel the energy of you.

Now as you breathe simply state:

On the inhale, quietly inside state: "I"

On the exhale, quietly inside state: "am."

When thoughts arise, curiously contemplate,
"Who is having these thoughts?"

Inhale: "I"

Exhale: "am."

FAITH IS INSIGHTFUL

When you feel a sensation in your body, curiously contemplate, "Who is feeling these sensations?"

Inhale: "I"

Exhale: "am."

When you are distracted by thoughts or sounds, curiously contemplate, "Who is distracted by these thoughts or sounds?"

Inhale: "I"

Exhale: "am."

Keep returning to the question of "Who am I?" and the simple answer of I am.

Inhale: "I"

Exhale: "am."

Be in the direct experience of "I Am," the energy of you.

> *When you are ready, take a deep breath and gently allow your eyes to open. Take out your journal and write about your responses:*

◈ What was your direct experience of the energy of you, the feeling of "Who am I"?

◈ Answer the question "Who am I?"

Do not edit yourself or try to get this answer right. Describe yourself as best as possible. Answer the question as if you were talking to a person you just met. Simply write whatever comes to your mind. Trust the answers, and write freely.

Individuals often define "Who am I?" by things such as career, interests, marital status, age, gender, appearance, and so on.

Faith knows there is so much more to you than all of these facts.

Return to your journal:

- Contemplate something that you truly love doing. You love who you are when you are doing it and love doing it so much time disappears. You feel fulfilled when you are taking part in this activity.

- Write down the qualities and characteristics of yourself when you are taking part in this activity. Does it fulfill you, allow you to be creative, adventurous, etc.?

- Now write down each of the qualities as a statement.
  I am fulfilled.
  I am creative.
  I am adventurous.

These are the qualities of the TRUE "I AM," the energy of you.

CHAPTER 5

Faith is the guidance power of the soul

*"Every heart has a divine intelligence and natural guidance
system. With every prayer, every meditation and every thought of
love, we tune in to ours." Marianne Williamson*

There is power in revealing your story and examining your life through the eyes of faith. Faith-filled understanding can transform the most difficult experiences into divine purpose. As a child, the voice of faith emerged and guided my family away from harm. Faith empowered me to stand up for myself and my family and move us out of harm. Within each of us is a guidance system: the divine intelligence of the soul. Our souls are equipped with faith, love, compassion, trust and all the things we need throughout the journey of life. The power of uncommon faith is to trust in guidance and act upon it without knowing why or how you will be able to. As a child, I did not question it, I trusted in it innocently. When I reflect on how I navigated through the difficulties in my life, I realize that this internal navigation system, the soul inside of me, was leading me all along. This GPS, the navigation system, is the *"Guidance Power of the Soul."*

Individuals often lose sight of their connection to the soul. Without this connection, an individual can feel alone and lost in world. This is often experienced as aimlessly moving from one place to another, one unfulfilling job to another or one relationship to another. When an individual loses sight of this connection, it is easy to succumb to the world and its troubles, forgetting who they truly are and what their divine purpose is. The guidance, the GPS is always available but not always accessed. Living in a state of disconnection is living lost and disempowered. When it feels like life has happened to you and that you are the only one who struggles, you can lose your way in life, get off course.

It is important to know that you are not alone. There is power in knowing that each of us has a story to tell, challenges to overcome and healing to do. Feeling lost and alone in the world is a state of disconnection. It is like having a computer that could access information and teach you things, but having no connection to the Internet. Without connection, this potential is just that, potential. Within you is potential, the capacity to learn from your story and no longer let that story dictate your life. If you free yourself from the story, the beliefs that hold you back, you can connect to the true "I Am." You can understand your story and your experiences through the eyes of faith. This transformative view of faith allows you to understand your past and past experiences in a way that transforms them into divine purpose.

Developing uncommon faith has been a major part of my personal journey ~ faith enough to act upon the guidance I receive by being bold enough to trust in it. Uncommon faith has been developed and matures each time I trust and follow my GPS. Uncommon faith is the connection to a deeper knowing, a knowing that guides an individual to the next purpose-filled step in life ~ the step needed in order to live in alignment with divine purpose. Uncommon faith is the action of taking those steps. At times, these steps don't make logical sense. You are asking "What am I here for?" and something new, something you have never contemplated before, shows up. This was my experience with yoga. I began to examine what am I here for, and the answer was yoga. It did not make sense, but my faith was strong enough and bold enough to follow it to the mat. When I began to slow down and get present in my life, I consciously brought my GPS back online.

This GPS system is always there and available to us; it is the divine intelligence of your heart and soul. Living in connection to this intelligence gives you access to the map for the journey of the soul, the orchestrated journey of your life. This map is tucked inside of you. Be willing to follow the guidance. Trust that if you follow the map you will arrive at your destination. Of course, just like with the GPS systems in cars, an individual can choose to take a different direction, to ignore the guidance. When an individual gets lost, they are off course. When you are using the GPS in your car, as long as you are going the right way, it is quiet, but as soon as you get off course, it speaks and will not silence until you are back on track. In the times of being tested, you may experience frustrations, disappointments, heartbreak and pain. Remain in faith and go online. Have faith that it will take you to the next experience you are meant to have in order to grow. Experiences that test you will also bring the most growth. Faith is the quiet voice at the center of your heart that encourages you to act, to move and trust in the directions that you are receiving. With faith, access your GPS and ask:

"What would you have me do here? Where would you have me go?"

At my clinic, I was experiencing a setback: Session numbers were down and it was my first year of boldly stepping out as the owner of a healing facility. I was struggling; feeling overwhelmed and I had gotten sick. I feared I had made the wrong decision. I was acting in faith, following the path. I was hitting a setback, or so I thought.

One morning I went in and sat in the space and asked, "How can I move forward? Show me what I do not see or may not be considering." As I sat quietly, I was guided to look up. There was a wall in front of me. I knew, in that moment, I had to take down that wall, let go of that treatment room, and create a class-room. It did not make logical sense; I was struggling financially. Where would the money come from? What about the income from that space? I chose to listen to the voice of faith.

Within two weeks, all was provided: supplies I could afford, assistance with the construction, and a beautiful classroom. This changed the entire situation and took away the strain on me. Faith spoke to me and I listened, and it came from a situation I perceived as a setback. With faith, this setback was transformed to set me up to begin offering classes at the clinic. These classes have proven to be a great asset, not only to the clinic, but all those who come through the doors and learn about alternative ways of healing. All I had to do was align to faith and the answers and direction were revealed.

Get back on track by reconnecting to faith, and accessing your GPS. Each day, renew your faith by making time for quiet, sacred time for prayer and connection. In order to get back on track, you have to listen, receive and follow the guidance. It may seem that it is taking you in the wrong direction, but faith would trust it. It just feels like a wrong direction because it is a new direction. It is a direction to a place you have never been and aren't familiar with.

I met Carla one evening at the yoga studio where I teach. At first I didn't even notice her. She seemed to melt into the backdrop of the lobby. I was closing out the day and preparing to go home. I felt this draw to look up and I noticed this young woman sitting shyly in the corner. I struck up a conversation with her just as I usually do with students in the studio. We began to talk about this and that: How long have you been practicing yoga? Where are you from? The normal getting-to-know-you dialogue. Then the conversation veered into energy, as it usually does with me. She asked if I was the teacher who had a flyer posted for an upcoming training on energy awareness. I said yes I was and had spaces open for this training and would she like to attend? Or did she have questions? She lit up and began to ask me questions and shared some personal information about why she wanted to attend. When Carla lights up, people notice, just as I did. When she lit up, I was immediately taken with her.

Carla is a beautiful, proudly tall, vivacious individual. She has a giant personality and love exudes from her when she is at her best. At this time in her life, she was not at her best. Carla grew up performing and modeling. When she stood up that night,

I was surprised by how tall she was. She had the energy of someone much smaller in size in all ways. She was withdrawn and I could sense she was missing something and desperately needed to find it. She had left part of herself behind somewhere along the way. She had lost faith in herself.

We began working together privately to prepare for the training and to do some personal healing work. Carla had recently moved back to Florida to live with her parents. She was going through a painful divorce. During the marriage there had been a lot of abuse on physical, emotional and mental levels. I could see the impression that this abuse had on her. At moments she would shine bright and then quickly retreat. She wanted to get back on her feet and find out who she was again. The effects of this marriage had changed her; she had lost confidence and faith in herself.

I guided her to explore: Is there a place within you that was not the abuse? Is there a place within you that you can connect to and have faith in again? Essentially I was asking her to rediscover the light that I clearly saw. I coached her along and assisted her in my role as healer. She worked to gently release the things keeping her from the clarity she was seeking. She knew she was strong yet she felt broken. It was time to realign her beliefs and restore her faith. She needed to restore her confidence so she could have confidence in her ability to make decisions. It was time to explore the next step. Not the place she found herself, but the place she is meant to be. This is faith: understanding that the difficulty may be where you are, but it is not where you are meant to stay. Carla knew she would stay stuck where she was unless she took action.

The action came at the level of uncommon faith. Her faith dared her to transform the stumbling block of an abusive marriage into a great stepping stone for her future. With faith, she realized that she could heal from the destruction of her marriage and move forward in victory. She could move forward stronger than she had ever known.

To this day, I have the privilege of witnessing Carla sharing her light with so many individuals. Carla is bold and daring and does what she loves in her life. She is a shining example of someone living on purpose and daring to take the earth walk of faith. As I helped her find her faith, Carla deepened my faith as well.

With faith all things are possible. ஓ

Faith-filled testimonial

"When I think back to the person I was when I met Felicia McQuaid in 2009, I am shocked at how far I have come through our work together in such a short amount of time. I set out on my journey of healing with Felicia after a very abusive marriage. This marriage had led me down a path of self-destruction and sabotage. I was guided to Felicia. Something told me I needed to seek out help from her, and I immediately booked my first appointment. Not knowing what I was even going to have done with my first treatment, I boldly came to her office, and my life was changed forever. Our work focused on forgiveness of myself and others, and healing my body, mind and spirit. This work led me down a path that has brought me more than just healing, but also purpose, peace and faith.

Faith in God was taught to me throughout my life, and faith in myself was always paramount in my family; however, the transformative work I have accomplished with Felicia has touched my soul in a way that integrated faith in both myself and the universe. The work we have done together has shown me that even in my darkest moments, faith emerges. A faith that comes from a deep-rooted understanding that all things will unfold just as they should, and that I am on my path to my highest, greatest and most authentic self. A faith that is constant and steady that allows me to dig even deeper into myself, knowing that the light at the end of the tunnel will always appear and at just the right moment.

I am successfully divorced from my abuser, and have found so much joy in relationships, work and myself. I am a reiki master teacher, a yoga teacher, and I completed a lifetime goal of being a director of development at a prominent children's charity during the time she has been my teacher, healer and friend. I have faith that I will continue

FAITH IS THE GUIDANCE POWER OF THE SOUL

to be led in the directions of my life purpose, because this faith I experience is no longer something I read about in a book or hear about from a religious leader; this faith is deep and rooted in the understanding that I am, that I am enough, that all is taken care of through this faith and that it all resides inside of me. This kind of faith is constant. It is a like a warm blanket just out of the dryer that makes your soul warm too.

Although I may still struggle with life, this faith continues to keep me steady even when life throws me a curveball. The work that Felicia continues to share with me, and the world, is life-altering in a deep and profound way. When one talks of faith versus doubt, I would say that after my work with Felicia, doubt has been completely replaced with faith.

Like a beacon from a lighthouse in a storm, Felicia has a way of showing me the way even when at first I could not see it on my own. Gently and with the utmost care and compassion, she has brought more to my life than I could ever express in words. The faith I have in myself and the universe is automatic now. I had a friend say to me, "Carla, it seems like everything just works out for you even when it seems impossible." This is true because of the work I have done with Felicia and the faith I have that it always will work out for me and my family, even when it seems impossible. This beautiful, effortless faith is a faith that is within me, a part of who I am now and thankfully through our continued work together will always be. A faith that is not written on a page, but lives inside of me. Thank you, Felicia, for being a beacon of love and faith for all who are fortunate enough to find you."

Carla M.

When you are courageous enough to listen and examine your life in new ways, the past is allowed to emerge, and the things you may have been suppressing come into the light. It is important to know that when these memories, these old wounds are revealed, it is good sign. It is the sign that you are strong enough to heal and ready for transformation. Faith encourages and guides you to heal and gives you the strength needed for this process. Faith is the voice inside that encourages healing and understanding. The energy of faith is needed now more than ever. When you step up to the path of healing, you will be guided in new ways. You may be guided to explore practices that heal. You may be guided to things like yoga, talk counseling, exercise, meditation, new books, new friends, forgiveness or reconciliation. The guidance is individual because it comes from your divine intelligence. It takes a degree of uncommon faith to have the courage to let the things that have been suppressed within you be revealed. Uncommon faith is the courage to act and take the necessary steps toward healing and the light of understanding.

Have faith in your ability and the strength you contain in order to examine your life. When someone does not have faith in themselves, guidance is doubted, and an individual doubts their capacity for change. Without faith, there seems to be no point to it all. Uncommon faith knows that all has purpose. Uncommon faith knows that each experience and person is meant to lead you toward your divine purpose. Suppressing memories, feelings and pain does not heal; it only allows them to be the underlying control of the unconscious. Things in the unconscious have a way of directing our thoughts and behaviors, but from a place of darkness. In the dark we fumble, we stumble and we continue to remain lost. In the light of awareness, things can be healed and examined from a transformative perspective. This happens by stepping forward and out of the dark and being bold enough to say, "Show me what I do not see and what I do not understand. I am strong enough to do what I need to do to be free."

When I stopped suppressing how I felt, true healing began. The painful memories I had buried deep inside were revealed, and true healing was possible. I could not heal what I would not feel or acknowledge. I thought I was leaving the past behind me, but I realized that if the past is not healed, it is still here in the present moment. I was merely ignoring it, sticking it in a dark room, and hoping it would just go away. I was waking up and realizing that I did not like where I was or how I was feeling, the feeling of disconnection. I had to investigate exactly where I was; I was at a crossroads. New things were standing before me; a new relationship, new friends, new teachers and new ways of being were being taught to me. I experienced a deeper call from within. I knew that in order to accept these new opportunities, to basically accept love, I had to make some important changes.

The first change, and the most crucial, was to get present. I needed to listen to my body, which was speaking loudly in the form of pain. I had prescriptions for depression and pain, but none of those things were helping. The pain pills only masked the pain; the depression pills only disconnected me and increased my sense of separation by numbing out the pain and myself. These feelings of disconnection and pain were the catalysts for my change. My faith knew that there is a way out of pain ~ that pain was not meant to be my day-to-day experience. My faith revealed that the anger I carried was harming me and chasing away everyone who was trying to love me. With faith, I decided I could no longer ignore the pain. I wanted to be free of the pain. I wanted to feel purposeful. I wanted to know who I was and what I was doing here. My life, from that moment on, has transformed and continues to transform. I had uncommon faith, the faith to make these decisions and take action. This commitment to healing, and having faith that I could heal, allowed my story to continue to unfold and be transformed.

> *"The secret to change is to focus all of your energy not on fighting the old but on building the new." Socrates*

So much time and energy in life is wasted focused on what is not working. When you focus your attention on what you don't like about yourself or your life, you become focused on unhappiness. Faith focuses on building the new and opens the door to change. Faith invites happiness in. A person of uncommon faith knows to place their focus and energy on what is wanted!

Allison walked into my office bent over in pain. You could see the pain in her eyes, hear it in her voice and it could be felt in the room as she entered. Immediately, I heard the word "unacceptable." It was completely unacceptable to see this powerful, beach-loving artist in so much pain. Allison is an amazing and talented artist; her artistry is her life. She is the owner of an art gallery where she shares her art and supports other budding artists. She is art and art is Allison.

Allison came to me searching for relief from her pain. The pain was creeping out of her body and slowly into every other aspect of her life. She was at the doorstep of back surgery and painful injections in search of relief. I love Allison's challenging and cynical style and I am equally amazed at her willingness to look at things truthfully and openly. This is what we did, and session by session, layer by layer, the pain lessened and healing happened.

With faith, Allison realized she needed to let go of anger and, with that, let go of pain. With faith, Allison experienced the beauty of discovering that everything was connected. She realized all she had to do was stand in connection to her life and then pain was no longer needed. Her pain had become the way of connection.

Faith-filled testimonial

"I was newly divorced with two kids and starting a new business while struggling with chronic back pain that started around the time of those life changes. The pain was so debilitating that it was literally painful for my friends and family to see me bent over while trying to "do life." I exercise a lot and love yoga and the beach life ~ these activities were all basically ground to a halt because of the pain, not to mention how hard my job as an artist and gallery owner became.

I heard about Felicia from some friends and thought I might as well give her approach a try since stretching, cortisone injections, yoga, sleeping, chiropractic adjustments, tequila, etc. weren't even touching the pain. We probably had five sessions before she noticed I was able to roll over on the table without wincing in pain and maybe 10 sessions before my pain level was down from a constant 8 to a 2.

The most important thing I've learned and actively live my life by is the importance of the mind-body connection. Without this connection, I was in pain and I now know it was the source of all my pain. I can't say enough how lucky I am to have found Felicia. With her faith-filled guidance and her expert care, my pain is gone. I continue to go and hand myself over to Felicia and try to soak in all I can learn about the healing process. Now that I understand the mind-body connection I am much better equipped to self-soothe and investigate my symptoms when something physical does arise. I can clearly identify what is happening mentally to trigger the physical symptoms and can take steps to remedy the problem. "Life-changing" is an understatement ~ for me, my friends, family and my kids! Thank you Felicia!"

Allison W.

Uncommon faith guides to you focus on the other side to the healing and transformation that is possible. Focus on the other side of pain, the other side of disconnection, the other side of unhappiness. The voice of faith is the guidance leading toward healing and transformation. Uncommon faith empowers you to explore and reveal what may be holding you back. Through investigation comes the freedom to heal, the freedom to change and the freedom to become who you truly are and do what you are truly meant to do. Living in a state of disconnection is living in suffering and struggle. Depression, anger and frustration arise when living in a state of disconnection and a life without purpose. An individual often loses sight of the path and their purpose without connection to and guidance from the GPS system, from their soul. Renew your faith daily, make time for quiet, make time for prayer, and make a conscious connection to the divine intelligence within your heart. Through faith, the guidance system is reconnected.

Having faith in yourself empowers you to follow the guidance that comes from your own intelligence, wherever that may lead you.

Apply the Lesson
GETTING IN TOUCH WITH YOUR GPS

Meditation:

Find yourself in a comfortable environment, some-where with minimum distractions so that you can be undisturbed for a period of time. Sit comfortably either on the floor or in a chair. If you are seated on the floor, have blankets or pillows under your bottom for support. If you are seated in a chair, either gather the legs under you or have the feet firmly planted upon the ground.

Sit with the spine straight, attentive to your posture. Place your hands lightly on your lap, palms facing up to signify openness. Let your eyes softly close and take a few moments to become quiet and attentive to the breath.

Bring your attention to rest deeply inside your heart, in the center of your chest. As your breath connects to your spiritual heart, it connects to your soul, the guidance power within you. As your attention rests deeply inside your heart, it brings your GPS online. Have faith in the guidance you receive when you are in connection to your heart and soul.

On your next inhale, quietly inside state: "Guide"

On your next exhale, quietly inside state: "me."

Repeat three times:

On your next inhale, quietly inside state: "Show"

On your next exhale, quietly inside state: "me."

Repeat three times:

Boldly, in faith, state the following intention for your day:

* "Today I will live from my heart and walk in faith."

* "I will make all my decisions in counsel with my inner guidance."

With faith all things are possible.

* "I will trust in the guidance I receive."

* "I will follow this guidance in faith."

* "Show me where to go."

* "Show me what to do."

When you are ready, take a deep breath and gently allow your eyes to open. Take out your journal and write down your responses:

Begin the day with this prayer and see where your guidance takes you.

* What does it mean to follow guidance?

* When I receive guidance do I trust it?

* When I receive guidance do I follow it?

* How do I receive guidance? (thought, feeling, hunch, gut instinct)

CHAPTER 6

Faith to reveal the story

"There is no greater agony than bearing an untold story inside of you." Maya Angelou

My mom, my brother and I arrived in Kansas to live with my grandparents, Helen and Lewis Heaton. Lewis was a "take no mess from anyone" kind of man, and Helen was the strong female who held down the fort and took care of everyone. Both had been in the dark about the abuse; I can only imagine my grandfather's reaction if he had known. They took us in without question and with love. They sheltered us from the storm of my father. They kept us safe. They fed us and gave us a place to live, but what I remember most about my grandparents is the love that they offered to us so easily and freely.

My grandmother has always been a source of strength for me, even now. She is in the spiritual realm, but she is always, at any moment, right next to me. She was a strong woman, a woman of faith, a woman of conviction and a woman whose main job in life was to take care of her family. She took care of my grandfather throughout her entire life. She dedicated herself as a mother to my mother, and she took care of us. I am so blessed to have had her in my life throughout my younger years. She was an anchor to me, the place where I knew without a doubt that I was loved. My grandfather was a strong, stubborn and loving man. I'm sure he's the reason that my father stayed away, why my mother was able to get away from my father. He took charge and helped us all to feel safe.

My mother attempted to start over; she left my brother and me to live with my grandparents as she went on and tried to start over for herself. We stayed behind and started school and saw my mother as often as we could. She moved to a bigger city to get

With faith all things are possible. ᎶᏜ

67

work and, I'm sure, to heal. She had to figure out who she was and what she needed to do.

I don't resent the time I spent with my grandparents. Those memories have always stayed alive within me: my grandmother putting me on a stool to help her to wash dishes, feeling like such a wonderful granddaughter with each pruning of my fingers. She gave me a cart small enough to carry one grocery bag. I wheeled my cart, at the young age of 6, across the street to the local store to pick up the supplies Helen had ordered moments earlier from the kitchen phone. These memories contain feelings of love and of having a safe place to live. Unlike our confined childhood in New York where we spent most of the time inside our apartment, my brother and I ventured off to historical parks and played on old cannons. Life in Kansas at this time was a place without all the yelling, without all the fighting and violence that formed our day-to-day existence in New York, living with my father, Felix. We are given plateaus throughout difficulty, places that allow for rest, integration and restoration, moments in which we are held, loved and cared for. The time with my grandparents was one of those plateaus for me.

The experiences with my father had a lasting effect. The pictures of me during this time change: I go from a happy, beautifully dressed and smiling young child into a girl who begins to put on weight, a girl who stops wearing pretty dresses and starts hiding, dressing tougher – a tomboy, if you will. She becomes a little more guarded and a lot more tentative around others. This young girl still feels everything very strongly and doesn't understand why or what to do with it.

My mother tells stories of when I was little, that when I was taken around others in my family, I would become ill. Most of the members of my family were older, and when we age, we tend to have one sickness or another. When I would be around those who were not well, I would pick it up. I believe it's the level of compassion and understanding I had at that age.

My soul wanted to help those who were struggling so much that I would unconsciously take on their pain and difficulty. Throughout my healing path, this pain and difficulty has been one of my greatest teachers, an indication of disconnection or suppression. I have learned to acknowledge it, heal it and cleanse it from the very cells of my body. The pain and difficulty are the messengers throughout my life that something is off and something needs to be cared for and attended to, just as the constant pain I was in at 28 years old got my attention to seek alternative ways to heal it.

We stayed with my grandparents until I was around 7. One day, my mother came and said we were moving back with her. She had met a man, they were going to get married, and we were all going to live together. I remember cautiously meeting this man, standing back, observing who he was, and observing my mother with this person. This man, Curtis, was noticeably younger than my mother, but he was a good man. Curtis exuded light and warmth. I remember him picking me up and placing me on his shoulders during that first meeting. He won me and my brother over very quickly with his love and with the joy that sparkled in his eyes. He was the definition of ease. Everything with Curtis was easy. He took us in as if we were his own. I could see that he loved my mother and that she loved him. My grandparents adored him as well, this man of Light.

Hope came alive inside me. I was hopeful that this would be the next great step for my family, the step that would bring us all back together, the step that would allow us to live with my mother again, and to possibly have a father. My own father was not allowed in the picture, to the point that my grandmother cut him out of all photographs. When I look at the few pictures we have from growing up, there are holes where his face used to be.

I see this as an indication of what I was being taught. I was being taught to ignore, cut out and break away from the pain, break away from those who cause you pain. There was no forgiveness. There was no compassion. It was as if we were being told to forget him, forget what had happened and move on. This is what many of us do: block out the past and try to forget it. But without forgiving it, it remains alive within us at an unconscious level. In the unconscious, it is guiding and directing thoughts, words and actions. It is a coping skill to ignore and move away from the people and things that cause pain, but unless you heal these things, you'll never really move away from them. You are tethered to them. You are bound to them. Many times the pain is felt physically. For many people, including myself, the body is the way we realize the pain that exists inside.

My mother and Curtis got married, and we moved into a two-story house in Strong City, Kansas. It really was a wonderful time; I felt loved and – dare I say? – happy. Of course, we had the normal struggles of family life, but I remember it as a time of happiness. Curtis was in the process of adopting us, making us his own children. Our family grew with the addition of my sister. I was 7 years old and had a new sister and a brother, a mother and a new father. Things seemed to be going very well for us; we were healing. We were enjoying our normal life; this plateau of love was so encouraging.

The sweetest memory I have is of one Christmas, waking up to sounds downstairs; sounds that I thought were Santa. I went to the stairs with my brother and saw Curtis and my mother laughing under a tree and setting up presents for us. That year, I received a Barbie on a motorized bike from Curtis, a.k.a. Santa Claus. Underneath the twinkling lights, a big-wheel tricycle awaited my brother. Barbie with her crazy little bike was one of my favorite gifts, and one thing that I truly remember as a sweet moment as a child. This would be our last Christmas with Curtis.

Life of ease was short-lived for my family. We were all home one morning, I was 8 years old, the doorbell rang, and standing at the door were two police officers. Curtis had been killed in a tragic car accident. A rush of cold filled me. I was standing there, again, that observant, empathetic and loving daughter with her mother as she received this devastating news. I remember the shock, the sharp pain, and my mother falling apart (little did I know how accurate this description of falling apart would be). My mother fell apart and broke in so many ways that day; the light and love she had found again after leaving my abusive father had once again been shattered inside her. She was lost, grief-stricken, angry at the world and alone again with her children. The hopes of our new life for my family were shattered in that moment.

My mother later shared with me that she was pregnant at that time with another child of Curtis'. She was so grief-stricken, so sick, that she lost this baby after just losing her husband. She lost the unborn son, she lost her husband and she lost herself on that day when we opened the door to those police officers. Life would never be the same. It could never be the same again. It was devastating for us all. No one knew what to do or how to be. My family, instead of pulling together, broke apart. I didn't know what to do or how to be. It was a shock; someone is there and suddenly never will be again. My sister never had a chance to get to know her dad; my heart breaks for her about this. She was only 6 months old when he passed. Curtis was such a good man, so kind-hearted, and so important to us all.

The next two years, after Curtis passed, became increasingly difficult. My mother fell apart. She began to drink to mask her pain. Our house was open to more and more people coming in and out. It was a home of chaos, filled with anger and grief. I stood in the center of all this, just an 8-year-old girl who was desperately trying to help and was desperately trying to take care of her brother and sister.

I know now that my empathetic and compassionate nature allowed me to absorb the pain of others. I did not know any other way to help but to take on the responsibilities of others. I began to take on the pain of others, to take on adult responsibilities and to take care of everyone around me. I was thrust into the role of mom. At 8 years old, I would leave school with my backpack on and ready with a stroller for my sister when I arrived at the sitter's to bring her home. I was thrust into the role of caretaker. I was thrust into the role of a grown-up at 8 years old, cleaning and preparing meals.

I lost the ability to play and be carefree. There seemed to be no time for play; I was lost in the chaos. I felt abandoned by my mother. I felt abandoned by everyone and everything. I felt like I was put in the spotlight, one that involved taking care of my brother and sister, cooking, cleaning and picking up my sister from the babysitter after school. I would come home, take care of my sister, change diapers, help prepare meals and keep an eye on my brother.

My mother fell and broke her hip. She was drinking so much. There were people around our house who were drinking with her. Oftentimes I would wake up during the night to a house full of strangers, billows of smoke and empty bottles. One night I woke up to the sound of police officers at my house in the middle of the night. I went out to see what was happening and found that my mother had put her fist through a window, broken it, and cut herself pretty severely. Among the adults drinking and smoking and taking various pills, I stood, wondering, "What is going on?" These were tough things to witness and, as a child, I could not understand it. No one ever sat down and explained anything to us; it was just the way things were. Since Curtis passed, it was the new norm of life. Ever increasing amounts of responsibility were thrust upon me.

My mother was lost in emotional pain, she was stuck, she felt abandoned, she felt angry, she felt lost and she felt grief-stricken. The energy of our body, especially in our legs and hips, is about feeling supported as we take steps in our life. It is about emotional maturity, and it is about feeling courage or fear, depending on where you put your focus. Since Curtis had passed, my mother was left unsupported; she was left with three children to take care of. Curtis had become the caretaker, the father, the husband, and her best friend. She had loved him so much that, later in her life, she had my sister and was carrying their second child.

The losses were so overwhelming that she got lost in them. She covered them with alcohol, drugs and men. She was unable to support herself, and, without faith, she had nowhere else to get support.

As a family, we had no open spiritual or religious connection. It was not spoken of; we did not pray or attend church on a regular basis. Our family motto, our family mantra, became "Shit happens" or "Life just happens." I heard this throughout my childhood - "Shit happens" - as if it was all random and we had no part in what was happening to us and around us. Looking back in the consciousness that I have now, I understand this was the only way my mother could explain all the difficulties that she and her family were experiencing.

In order to change any of it or to deal with it differently, she needed the courage, strength and faith in order to meet these challenges. She would have had to look to something greater, to look to her faith, a relationship with the divine/God, a relationship with herself, and trust. If she had the understanding that life was not just randomly happening and that she had a part to play in it, this understanding would have asked her to have faith and know that she could handle any challenge that was there before. This was not the case.

Without faith, the world seems to have no order: Good things happen; bad things happen. We have no control over any of it. Good things happen randomly, bad things happen randomly, without faith there is no order. This is the understanding of many. This was definitely what was taught in my own home. My family did not have a deep spiritual or religious connection and, as such, no understanding of the divine order and purpose to life. Faith is the understanding that all has divine purpose.

I know I came with a deep understanding of faith. I believe it is inside of each one of us, a place inside to hold steadfast in the most difficult places. In the midst of all the chaos, I have often wondered, "Why? Why don't the adults around me change things? This can't all be random." I could see choices that were being made around me. I could see that these choices were playing a part in the experiences we were all having and the life that was going on around us.

I did not buy into this belief; I would not adopt it as my own, this idea that things just happen and that we are powerless to do anything about it. Uncommon faith is what I came here to develop and learn more about in this lifetime, on this journey. This uncommon faith has been the framework of my life, even when I wasn't conscious of it. I know this level of faith is what empowered me as a child, amid the chaos, to be able to rise up and to do what needed to be done daily.

As an adult, I once had a dialogue with my mother during a period of reconciliation. We talked about whether the acts of one made a difference to others. I know and have always known without a doubt that the acts of one make a huge difference to others. My mother strongly disagrees. She holds on to the belief that life happens to her, that life happens to us, and we are powerless in that process. I do not believe this; I see how each thing I do has an effect on everyone around me. This effect can be uplifting and positive, when I am in the right state of consciousness and sharing my light in the world, or it can be negative, bringing others down when I choose to only share my fears, judgments and inadequacies. I think of the profound effect that my grandparents, especially my grandmother, Helen, had on me. Her love and support kept faith alive in me. I see how this one person, being a constant in the backdrop of my childhood, was my saving grace. When I would need love, and someone to trust, she would always love and believe in me.

From 8 to 12 years old, I saw some of the most challenging times I've ever experienced. To this day, a deep hurt sometimes still rises in me that says, "I can't do it. I can't take one more thing!" I thought this regularly during those times. In healing, that little girl would often ask me, "When is the time for play?" In my personal healing work, I've often had to take her to the park and swing. I've often had to pull out the crayons and the watercolors and explore creativity, because those are the things she missed and wanted as a child.

When I was nearly 10, my mother remarried in the living room of our home in Emporia, Kansas. She married a man who lived next door to us, whom she had started spending time with. This was a time when there was still a lot of drinking and drug use. I remember him spending more time with my mother and with us as well, then suddenly, a Justice of the Peace was marrying them, and we were all eating cake. This new stepfather would prove to have a deep impact on my life.

I often wonder if there was a part of me as a child that hoped things were going to get better. I am not sure it was there this time. I had been hopeful for Curtis, and that did not turn out so well. It felt more like, "OK, let's see what happens now. Will this marriage bring stability and support?" My mom was hopeful that things could get easier for all of us. This did not prove to be the case.

The abuse started the night they married. My stepfather had moved into our home prior to the marriage, but just for a short period of time. But the night of their wedding, he snuck into my room and crossed boundaries with me. In my healing path and my personal journey of healing, I've come to realize that, prior to this first conscious remembering of sexual abuse, there had been others, that during the chaotic times prior to this marriage others had crossed boundaries with me and had done harm to me, but those I did not recall until much later and were one-time occurrences. This was different.

I do recall this night, and how it affected me so deeply. At 10, I was a precocious, strong-willed, overweight and stubborn child. I was desperate for attention, desperate for love and desperate to be seen. My stepfather took advantage of those needs. He saw me, but not in ways that I needed. I did not understand what was happening. There were times I wondered if I was dreaming. He only came into my room at night, and it wasn't every night. I internalized it is as my own fault, for I needed love and attention. I wanted someone to see me, and because of that, I had believed it was my fault that my stepfather was abusing me. I did not tell anyone what was happening. I did not tell anyone for years to come. He made sure to tell me that no one would ever believe me, that if I told my mother it would be me she would get rid of, not him.

I often wondered how my mother did not see what was going on. How did she not know when he was gone in the middle of the night and where he was? How did she not see the effect it was having upon me? How could she not see?

Now I understand how she did not see. She could not see. She would not see, for if she did, what would she have had to do? She would have had to choose to start over again. She would have had to acknowledge that things again were falling apart, deeper and deeper, around her, that things were more broken than she wanted to admit. She would have had to admit that she brought this person into our home, and that this person was causing great harm to her daughter. She could not admit or see what was going on.

My mother worked a lot during that time. She had gotten her degree in nursing and spent many nights and days away on long shifts, which left us home with my stepfather. Throughout those years, the abuse came and went. There were times when nothing would happen, and I would hope and wonder if it was over. But then, as quickly as I wondered that, it began again. The abuse seemed to correlate with my mother's work schedule. The more she was gone; the more it happened. Years passed, and by the time I was 10, my stepfather openly discussed what he was going to do when my mother wasn't around, winking at me or grabbing my legs while my mother washed the dishes. At that point, the abuse had moved outside of the confines of my bedroom. I never felt safe or comfortable. I lived in a constant state of anxiety, sadness and anger about what was happening to me.

The angrier I become, the more acted out. I secretly hoped someone would see past the anger, into the pain, and see what was happening to me in my own home. I put on weight. It was a form of protection on an unconscious level: a way to make myself less attractive, to hide inside myself more. I carried this weight with me well into my adult life. The weight gain had started at 4, the first time I experienced abuse. The weight became a metaphor for the pain I was carrying from each experience of abuse, each trauma.

I made a choice not to tell anyone about the abuse, thinking I was protecting my little sister and my brother. It was just as I had done with my own father, standing in front of him when he was turning his abuse on others. I was standing in front of them and taking the abuse, in hopes it would stop with me. I decided not to tell anyone for fear that, as my stepfather was telling me, no one would believe me.

When a child is not guided, not loved, not cared for or made to feel safe, she is not sure what to do with her experiences. As a parent now, I look at my children and wonder, "How did I do it?" It has been a miraculous process, to break the family chain of abuse and unworthiness. Thankfully, my own children came into my life after I started the healing process. I wanted their experience as a child to be one as a child.

I can't imagine my sweet daughter, who is almost 8, being thrust forward into those roles, into those responsibilities, and to encounter that type of abuse. It breaks my heart to think of such things. The uncommon faith I have inside me has always been my saving grace. Uncommon faith contains the power of grace and is the guidance I have followed to allow me to heal deep family patterns. As I have transformed and healed, these experiences have become my strength. They have become strength in the form of resilience, dedication, courage, understanding, forgiveness and, ultimately, compassion. I have learned deep compassion for that beautiful golden-haired girl. I have learned to transform her anger with compassion. I have learned to transform her fear with faith and compassion. I have learned to share compassion for her heart and, in so doing, transform the pain.

The sexual and physical abuse went on for years in my home; it became normal in my life. As I grew older, it became increasingly difficult for me to hide and to experience this abuse. I knew it was wrong, and at the same time I was told that no one would believe me. I was told that I had allowed it, and I believed it was my fault. It had been going on for so long now, how could I tell someone? How could I let this truth come out? I knew that when I did, if I did, life would fall apart in a whole new way. Things would fall apart not just for me, but for my whole family. When truth rises to the surface, it brings with it light and shows all things. When and if this truth came to the surface, it would put a spotlight on the things going on behind closed doors.

At the age of 11, things became the most difficult for me, and it became crucial for me to get help. I voiced my refusal to allow the abuse to continue. I challenged my abuser, I challenged my mother, and I challenged my life. I acted out – staying out later with friends that my mother did not approve of, arguing and fighting with both my stepfather and mother. I asked for help by acting out. It was the only way I knew how. When I later asked my mother about this time, she said that to her I seemed like a rebellious child, not a child who was in pain. She dismissed what she saw as a child who wanted attention by acting out. I wonder why she didn't look deeper. I had been the child who was so responsible, the child who was helping all the time in so many ways. To acknowledge my pain and struggles would have forced my mother to acknowledge the pain and struggles of our family.

One night, my mother was away on one of her long shifts as a nurse, and my stepfather came to me, and I refused. I was done. At this stage, I was making his life more difficult, not being asleep when he crept into my bedroom, being fully awake and ready to challenge him. I told him I was going to tell someone. I was going to tell my mother what was going on, because I wasn't going to allow it anymore. I wanted him to leave me alone. He refused, tried to force himself on me, so I ran. He pinned me down to the floor with scissors to my neck and said if I told anyone he would hurt me. "Tell anyone, and they won't fucking believe you. Tell anyone; I'll slit your throat." I was terrified. I was more scared of the cool steel of those scissors against my throat and the distinct possibility of him killing me than I was of telling someone about the years of abuse. But I got away from him that night and knew that it was time to reveal what was going on.

A few nights later, my mother took me to work with her. I was in the break room with one of my mother's friends, and I was emotionally distraught. I'm sure an outsider could see that I was in pain. I feel like this moment was divine intervention. I needed to tell someone who would understand and believe me. I told her what was going on. I told her that it had been going on for a long time, I told her of the experience a few nights before with the scissors. She believed me and took action where I could not. Things changed very rapidly from that moment forward.

This woman would not allow me to go home. She believed me so strongly that she called social services, and they entered the situation. I was almost immediately moved out of my home and put into the foster care system. I was 11 going on 12. I was taken from one situation in my home that was difficult, and I was moved into foster care.

Even though I was taken away from the abuse at home, foster care was also very difficult. I spent close to two years in foster care. I had adapted to the difficulty of home life, and now I was in foster care and I didn't know what to do. Being in a foster home was like being a number. In the foster home I was placed in, children came and went frequently. Some children stayed for a night or two, others stayed for a week or two, and others stayed for a few months. The children came and stayed for different amounts of time, and they also came to the foster home for a number of reasons.

My first night in the foster home, separated from my mother, brother and sister, I stayed up all night crying and wondering if I'd made a huge mistake. I wondered if it had been the right decision to tell. Now I know it was the only thing I could've done. It was the only way I could escape the abuse. It was the first of many steps in this journey from difficulty to divine purpose. I had to leave my brother and my sister behind, and I was moved into the next place on my path. My heart and mind were trying to make sense of the fact that I was in this new place, with strangers, and unsure of what would happen next. Although I was surrounded by children in similar situations, I felt so alone. This place was so unfamiliar. The people were so unfamiliar. There is an old saying that I think about often:

"Better the devil you know than the devil you don't." Jack Heath

The difficulty that we know how to deal with is often chosen because we don't know how we would deal with the next thing, the next difficulty. There is a fear the next thing will be even more difficult. When life has been one difficult experience after another, you start to believe that is all there is. Life can seem like a series of difficult events, with nothing good coming. Without faith, you may get lost in the difficult experiences and lose hope. Faith knows there are good things to come, that where you are is not where you are meant to be. As a young girl, there had been moments of good inside the difficulty I experienced, but they were always short-lived. My reality was one of struggle, pain and sheer difficulty. Without connection to faith, I felt lost and alone.

As I laid on the bottom bunk in an unfamiliar room on that first night in foster care, I heard the cries of the girl above me. She was a German girl who had come in a few days before me. As she cried, she screamed out curse words in German. The only one I could make out was "shiza," or "shit" My family belief system or motto had followed me here to the foster home. "Shiza, shiza, shiza ... shit ... shit ... shit ..." She was screaming what my heart was saying and what my mind had come to believe: Shit was happening again.

I felt disconnected from everything and everyone. No one talked to me; no one counseled me. After my initial interview, no one asked about the abuse again, and I lived in a house with other foster children. I felt isolated, on an island of misfit toys, except I couldn't trust the other toys, so anger became my only friend. When we feel alone, it is ultimately because we feel disconnected from the source of faith. Faith is a knowing and a trust that we are never alone and always being guided purposefully through each experience on our journey. All I felt connected to were the feelings of heartache, abandonment and pain. My faith was buried under the voice of pain and it became hard for me to hear and feel.

There is a process to the foster care system. I was going to be there for a while. I was enrolled in a nearby public school in a larger city about an hour away from where I lived, and I did my best to fit in and adapt to this new environment. I had no choice. It was where I was and what had to be done. No matter the difficulty I was going through, I still had school to attend and homework to do. I tried to figure out how to do this in foster care. I didn't have a lot of friends. Everyone knew who the foster kids were, and they stayed away. While things were sorted out, I was kept separated from my entire family. I was more afraid, confused and angry than I may ever truly understand. How was it that I was the one who was being hurt and abused, and yet I was the one who was cast out? I had no contact with my family, including my brother and sister, except in court or monitored visits.

Court was an excruciating experience. I had to take the stand in front of a room full of strangers, including my mother, and reveal what had been going on. My mother showed up at court with him, supporting him. I had to reveal the abuse that had I concealed for so long. It was humiliating, and the more I had to reveal, the more shame and blame I felt, and I had to reveal it to my stepfather and my mother who was by his side. To carry the story inside was one thing, but to say it out loud was something else. When I spoke of the abuse, I was the abuse. I had adapted to the abuse, and the abuse had become my identity.

After I told my side of the story in court, my mother took the stand. I had hoped and prayed she would believe me. Despite the fact that she was holding his hands minutes prior as I divulged how he slipped into my bedroom for years, I hoped she would stand up for me. She would see the truth and apologize, and I would have my mother back. Instead, she thought that I was making it all up. She stood in court that day and told the world I was a troubled child and a liar. She gave no importance to me or my experience as a child being abused in her home. It was as if she had taken those scissors, the catalyst to all of this, and slit my throat. She betrayed me so deeply; that wound took many years to forgive and overcome.

My deepest fears had come to life. I had held the story in so long because my abuser was telling me no one would believe me. The one person I needed to believe me and believe in me, my mother, could not and would not hear. I was around 13 years old and being told that what I was going through and what I had gone through was a lie. It was devastating. But it was the reality I faced.

I became very angry and lost, and had lost confidence in love. The one person who was meant to love me above all else, in spite of everything, betrayed me. I was expected to go on with life, to adjust to new surroundings and my new school. The foster home was in a constant state of flux. There were different children in and out of the home on a regular basis. I received no guidance, no counseling and with that no under-standing. My essential needs were being met, such as a place to rest, food and education, but no real sense of love, compas-sion and understanding. The only companion I had, and it would continue to be my companion for quite some time, was the anger that I felt. I stayed in foster homes for the next two years. I rarely saw my family and didn't feel connected to the family I was staying with.

I know what I truly wanted was to feel connected and loved. I felt like I had nothing and no one. I wonder if this despera-tion for connection made me vulnerable to abuse. While away one weekend with my foster family, one of the relatives of the foster family forced himself on me. On Memorial Day weekend, which is also my birthday, this relative crossed boundaries with me. In a place I had come to escape the abuse, abuse found me again. It was hard to believe, so much so that I blocked this experience from my memories until my late-30s.

For years, I struggled with deep depression on or around my birthday. Even when I was surrounded by love and people who loved me, I fell into this place of sadness. I had always just contributed it to my past, but did not understand how deep this pain was. I understand now that forgetting, suppressing and denying were the only ways I knew to survive and function. It was what I was taught to do. It was the belief system I had learned, one that says, "Bury it and pretend." When you really start wanting to live a life of purpose and trust in the power of faith, this is no longer acceptable. From the inside out, the soul must free itself of lies.

I shared with my foster family what happened while we were away. They knew I had already been accused of lying. They knew I was troubled and angry, so how could my word be trusted? To have a similar situation occur in a place I was supposed to be safe amplified the anger inside, and I felt more and more alone. I wanted out; I missed my siblings, and I wanted a way out. I betrayed myself and told everyone I lied about everything, the abuse at home and the abuse in the foster home. I was so confused and angry; I just didn't care and thought if I could get home I would figure it out from there.

I was so persuasive that I convinced everyone I had lied about it all. At this point, what did I have to lose? I was abused at home, and here I was in foster homes being blamed again for abuse that occurred to me. I thought, "If I can get home, I can figure it out for myself." Soon I was sent home. I was angry, broken, lost, and most of all, afraid. Going home was strange. I was coming home based on a lie, and I knew it. My mother and I had not been in contact much, and I had not seen my siblings for a long time. I had no idea what had been going on while I was away. I'm sure they did not understand either.

The very first night of my return, my stepfather came to the door of my bedroom. It was déjà vu. How had I found myself back here again? I was older, and my anger was not going to tolerate the same experience beginning again. I used the anger to protect myself; I used the anger to keep him and everyone away. It was the only thing I knew how to use. It was the only thing that was real to me. The anger became my protector, my best friend, and the only thing in which I had faith. I had faith in my ability to use anger to keep others away, and it was very effective. He attempted to abuse me again, he bullied me, convinced my mother to be against me, but the abuse never happened again. I spent most of my time being out of the house.

Life went on. We all did the best we could. My family masked the past by ignoring it: Don't talk about it, it didn't happen, and it wasn't real. It was easier to bury the pain than be truthful about it. This is what I was taught. This is what I knew. So the pain and the anger were buried deep inside of me. It became part of my very existence. It became a part of the cells of my body. It became a part of my thoughts and it became the self that I knew. I remember times when I had great outbursts of anger. I found myself screaming and hitting things until my hands and arms bled. If anyone got close to me, I found a way to hurt him or her. Something inside me said, "Hurt them before they hurt you."

I had no sense of direction and felt so disconnected from everything. Living disconnected from faith left me feeling lost and alone. I know now that faith has always been inside of me as it is inside of everyone. Faith is always there, sitting patiently waiting inside of you. I realize now that faith offers guidance at all times; whether this guidance is followed or tuned into is up to us. Faith is the loving energy inside the heart of us all and, if you trust in it, it will guide you from experience to experience. During the difficult times of my life, it was the guidance and the knowing moved me. My GPS, my soul, in each moment, is always lovingly guiding me toward what I need to do and where I need to go. This faith, the same knowing I had experienced so innocently at 4 years old, arose again and guided me to move to the next place on my journey. Uncommon faith guided me to leave home.

At 16 years old, I knew I needed to get away from my home environment. Maybe then, I thought, I could figure some things out on my own. This knowing – the knowing that it was time to take the next step – came from the voice of faith. Faith is so beautiful that it guides us even when we don't know where the guidance is coming from.

With faith all things are possible. ⬤

I had enough sense to continue to go to school. I'd always been a good student and knew that completing school was important. I moved into a dorm-like home, where I had a small room and a safe place to lay my head at night. I worked two jobs, waitressing at a hilltop café on weekends and a neighborhood Sonic a couple of nights during the week, and I went to school. Granted, I engaged in some self-destructive behavior, smoking pot and drinking until I blacked out, but I was still responsible enough to hold down two jobs, take care of myself and finish high school on my own. I was still that 8-year-old with the backpack and stroller.

I graduated with my class, but at graduation no one was there for me. I was disconnected from everyone in my family. My grandparents had long passed and I was alone. I remember crossing the stage in cap and gown. I shook the hand of the principal, diploma in my other hand. Some of the students before me hoisted their diplomas overhead to cheers from the audience. I looked into the crowd, thinking, "Surely, someone has got to be out there." No one. After the ceremony, boys and girls trickled off into groups, surrounded by friends and family, snapping photos, laughing. I took one look around and walked to my car. The first thing I did when I got back to my little room was peel off that cap and gown and proceed to go out and get wasted. I have no idea how I got home that night. The car was caddy-cornered into a parking spot; vomit was on the floor. And I was alone. The only person I could have faith in and rely on was me.

I floated around for the next few years. Increasingly, I turned to drugs and alcohol, promiscuity, and shallow relationships with anyone who would pay attention to me. I simply survived. I floated around from job to job, in and out of relationships. Nothing lasted very long. I drank until I blacked out and then experienced fits of rage. My anger was my constant companion.

When I was 18, I was introduced to a young man who showed interest in me. I became hopeful that this relationship would last. I was hopeful that this relationship would be something I could count on. We had a short, passionate courting. We would fight and make up, fight and make up; this is what I thought love was. It was the only kind of love I had ever known. One weekend, rather than break up, we decided to get married.

Before the marriage ceremony, as I sat in my car, a voice arose inside of me saying, "Don't do it. This is not the right thing for you." I realize now this was the voice of faith, the voice of divine guidance. This guiding power came from within, but I tried to ignore it. I wanted someone to love me. I sat in my car, hardly able to breathe, paralyzed, hearing this voice saying, "Don't do it." It was as if a part of me would not allow me to go inside and marry this person. The voice of faith and the power of it were attempting to hold me there, and I knew in my heart the voice was right. What was I doing, driving in my crappy car to a friend's home to stand before a Justice of the Peace and marry a man whom I didn't really get along with? "What if this is it? What if this is my only chance at love?" Fear had gotten the better of me. Fear of being alone. Fear of not being loved. This man loved me. Wasn't that what love was: drama and fighting? Once again fear and faith exchanged words, and I chose not to listen to the voice of faith, my internal guidance.

It didn't take long for this relationship to turn abusive. I'm sure much of the anger that I carried brought out the anger in him. I pushed. I tested. In a way, I wonder if I was proving myself right, if I was proving the angry part of me right, the part that knew everyone was going to hurt me. Our fighting escalated to the point of physical abuse. I was in this familiar place again. I knew this place all too well, the place where shit happens, and the place where I accepted less than. I had learned to equate abuse with love. I placed myself in harm's way and I knew it, but did not know how to leave the abuse.

My family decided to move to North Carolina to "start over." I had no plans of joining them. I was married and had a life in Kansas; not the ideal life, but life as I knew it. Two nights before my family was due to leave, I woke up in the middle of the night to a voice from within that said, "If you stay here, this is the life you choose." Unable to catch my breath, I lay sweating next to the man who days before pinned me down on the bed and left black and blue marks against my backside, contemplating "If you stay here, this is the life you choose." My family was leaving. They were my people; if they were gone, I had nothing but my husband, no one to turn to if things got really ugly. Is this what I wanted for myself? Is this all I deserved? I made a decision to leave. I knew I had to follow this guidance and take a leap of faith. I had no idea what was waiting for me in North Carolina or what I would do there. I did know I could not stay and could not choose this life. I left without telling my husband. Similar to the night in New York when my mother, brother and I escaped on the bus, I left most of my possessions behind. With no room in the passenger area, I rode in the back of a U-Haul with the furniture and followed that guiding power of faith to the next stop on my journey, one step closer to my destiny. It was an act of uncommon faith.

What makes a 4-year-old know enough to call for help, even when her mother could not or would not call for help? What gave me the courage to move across the country based on a voice and knowing? What guided me to reveal the abuse that led me to foster homes? What saved me time and time again from would have been further harm? I know it to be faith, the GPS of the soul.

An individual has an opportunity, with each decision they make, to listen to this guidance. Your whole life is about choices you make; either choosing to follow the guidance of the soul or living lost in the world. Uncommon faith chooses to listen to the guidance of the soul, even in the most difficult times. Uncommon faith knows you are being watched over. Uncommon faith knows nothing happens without a purpose. Acting in faith, you realize that you are strong enough to handle any situation that stands before you. Uncommon faith knows that within you is everything you need to overcome any challenge and triumph over any situation. Uncommon faith is a knowing that is unbreakable and unmistakable. In these moments, each time you are brave enough and faithful enough to act upon this guidance, to move away from fear and always toward faith, it takes you one step closer to your destiny, your ultimate destination.

This guidance system, the map of the soul, guides an individual through each of the challenges and each situation experienced in life. The soul mapped this journey out upon your conception and knows where you will end up, what difficulties you will face, and it knows the divine purpose of each situation. The soul knows the purpose of each person you've encountered and each experience you've had. Have faith in this truth. You are not dropped off on this planet and abandoned without a map, without a guidance system built into you. When you feel lost, abandoned or unsure of which direction to go, tune into your personal GPS system and say, "Show me where to go, what to do next."

> *Having faith in the guidance within you, your personal GPS system, allows you to trust in the guidance you receive from it; ultimately you learn to trust and faith in yourself.*

❦ Apply the Lesson
GETTING IN TOUCH WITH YOUR STORY

Meditation:

Find yourself in a comfortable environment, somewhere with minimum distractions so that you can be undisturbed for a period of time. Sit comfortably either on the floor or in a chair. If you are seated on the floor, have blankets or pillows under your bottom for support. If you are seated in a chair, either gather the legs under you or have the feet firmly planted upon the ground.

Sit with the spine straight, attentive to your posture. Let your eyes softly close and take a few moments to become quiet and attentive to the breath. Simply breathe and with each breath become ever more quiet and connected. Simply breathing in and simply breathing out.

Allow your mind to travel back, back in time to a place in your life that was difficult for you. Allow the memories to come forward and the feelings to freely flow. Know that you are safe here in the present moment as you explore the memories of the past.

Notice how your body feels as this memory comes forward on the screen of your mind. Notice your emotions as this memory comes forward on the screen of your mind. You are safe, as you simply observe this memory as it comes forward on the screen of your mind. Stay gently connected to your breath and the simple in-flow and out-flow, the rhythm of your breathing. Watch this memory unfold as if you were watching it on the movie screen of your mind. Know that you are safe.

Continue in this way for 5 to 10 minutes. You are safe in the present moment to observe this memory as it unfolds on the screen of your mind. The breath flows in, the breath flows out. The memory is allowed to arise fully and completely as you simply observe and breathe.

From this observer state of awareness, the true
"I Am," contemplate:

- What could be a greater purpose, a divine purpose for this difficulty?

- What did I learn from this situation?

- What strength could it have been developing?

- Simply ask the questions without attachment to the answer.

When you are ready, take a deep breath,
bringing your full attention back to the
present moment. Gently allow your eyes
to open. Take out your journal and write
about your responses:

- What memory came forward?

- What could be a greater purpose, a divine purpose for this difficulty?

- What did I learn from this situation?

- What strength could it have been developing?

CHAPTER 7

Faith in something new

"Blessed are the cracked for they shall let in the light."
Groucho Marx

Where you have been is not where you are meant to stay. Like me, you may have experienced pain, trauma, tough times, heartbreak, betrayal, anger and unfair circumstances. I have faith that these experiences are not meant to be the legacy of my life. Rather, by acting in faith, these experiences are just the beginning. These experiences sometimes crack an individual open and lead them to believe that they are broken and defeated. Remember the wonderful fact that beliefs are not always the 100-percent truth. Beliefs can change, they can be re-examined, and you can redefine yourself and your past. You may have experienced pain and heartbreak, but that is part of the exquisite journey of life. Just because you have experienced loss does not mean you are alone. Just because you have experienced sadness does not mean you are meant to live in depression. Rise up in faith and know that you are meant to be happy, you are meant to be fulfilled, you are meant to know love, and you have a purpose to serve. When you change, your beliefs are realigned to faith-filled understanding. Uncommon faith knows with certainty there is something greater meant for this one precious life. A person of uncommon faith uses the old stumbling blocks of the past as the stepping stones to greatness. Examine the past in a new context, through the understanding of faith. Be willing to ask what divine purpose the difficulty contains. Could it be the soul's journey to triumph?

Don't let the past be the obstacle to your future; instead, shift your understanding of it so it empowers you. Make stepping stones out of stumbling blocks. Release those old beliefs, the ones that tell you that because of the past, you cannot be successful, you are not worthy of good things and you will be unable to achieve your goals. Those old beliefs will keep you stuck. Uncommon faith tunes out those doubts and fears. It is the voice of encouragement and optimism. Your faith will guide you toward all good things. Your faith will guide you to make necessary adjustments in order to live a life of purpose.

Without faith, there can be a lot of thinking about making changes, but most likely not a lot of action. With just a mustard seed of faith, the uncommon-degree level of faith, the necessary steps required to achieve goals become easier to take. The encouraging voice of faith always guides you through each step along the way. Your voice of faith may be guiding you to a new career or relationship, or simply to heal so you can live a happy, purpose-filled life. When faith is lacking, it is hard to trust that things could work out and life could be different. A person of uncommon faith dares to take action even when there is fear. With faith, new things are possible, all things are possible. Uncommon faith is letting go of who you believed yourself to be, and becoming who you truly are. Uncommon faith is willing to let go of what you have believed about your life in order to transform into what it is meant to be. A person of uncommon faith seeks to stand in the light and understand who they are, what they are here for and what they are truly capable of.

In depression, Lauren could not show the world her light. She had a hard time seeing it herself. Lauren was losing faith in herself. The years of depression were visibly noticeable, as if she was wearing a coat that was too big and heavy for her. Lauren is one of the most amazing people to know. She is this wild, curly headed, adorable soul that I knew that I could help. I had faith that when Lauren healed and as she healed that her light would be a ray of hope and healing for everyone she meets. Her divine purpose is to heal so she can guide others to their own light.

Lauren had endured a difficult childhood that followed her everywhere she went. Our work transformed her perceptions of the past, gave her faith that the struggles had divine purpose. Lauren empowered herself to look at these experiences through the lens of faith. The lens of faith gave her the ability to not only connect to the difficulty of the experiences but connect to the beauty and purpose contained within with those experiences. Lauren believed she was depressed because of the past. In actuality her depression came from not living in the light of who she truly is. She had come to believe she was the past, she was the depression, and she lost faith in herself.

Faith-filled testimonial

"When I first came to Felicia, my ability to recognize that I was worthy of love was painfully clouded, my understanding of faith shaky. Depression came and went in my life, leaving me unable to find who I truly was. I always questioned if I had somehow missed my life purpose. Felicia created a sacred space to uncover my true essence. Within each healing session, a cloudy layer fell away. I began to understand my pattern of turning my anger inward toward myself. This caused a deep sense of self-hatred and unworthiness, ultimately showing up as depression. As we worked together to clear this pattern through divinely guided energy healing, I was shown that I am always supported and in the presence of God. We just have to ask, let go of how it will come and see what unfolds in our highest good. Through this process, I now have a solid understanding of pure Faith. Living daily, knowing I am unconditionally loved and lovable, I can now see my divine purpose clearly. It has not been missed, but perfectly orchestrated. Felicia was the Earth Angel who held my hand as I walked over the bridge in Faith to my authentic self."

Lauren R.

It is possible to change your view of the cracks and to see those situations that cracked you open as a means to let out your light and to let some light in. To let light into a situation is to become en-"light"-ened. Changing your view is to move away from the darkness. Darkness, in a spiritual context, is ignorance. It is a state of not knowing and not understanding. Allowing light in through the cracks is the way of wisdom, the way of faith. You may believe you are broken because things have cracked you open, but what if you knew these cracks were to let light out and let light in? Beliefs are opinions or judgments that an individual has fully invested in and has come to know as truth.

> *"A belief system is nothing more than a thought that you've thought over and over again."* Wayne Dyer

Invest in something new. Invest in faith. Faith will allow you to see yourself in new ways; faith will allow you to see your life in a new way. Empower yourself to change your opinions and beliefs about yourself and the past. Uncommon faith allows for something new. Faith is not about beliefs, opinions or judgments; faith is more powerful than beliefs. If you believe you can, or you believe you can't, you limit yourself around that belief. Faith is unlimited. With faith, all things are possible, so what does that leave out? Faith is an expansive energy; beliefs are limited. At one time, people believed the world was flat. Then a few courageous souls had enough faith to test this belief. They had faith that when they arrived at the horizon line, the waters would continue and there was more beyond what they could see and knew for sure.

With faith, beliefs are transformed and re-aligned to truth.

Limiting belief	*With faith*
I am unlovable.	I am love and loveable.
I am not beautiful.	All of life is beautiful, including me.
Things just happen in life.	There is divine purpose to everything.
I am not good enough.	I am perfect and loved just as I am.
I am broken.	I am whole, perfect in my imperfections.

FAITH IN SOMETHING NEW

When I began to challenge and investigate my own beliefs, my life began to shift dramatically, all around me. When I let light in, I simultaneously began to feel lighter. I examined the past in a way that revealed and released the harmful beliefs I continued to invest in. With faith, I understand the experiences of my past taught me powerful things and had made me strong and resilient. I was learning about compassion, forgiveness and the power of faith. I was learning about the purpose and order of each experience in life. I wasn't broken unless I stayed in that belief. I had faith in what I was learning. I had faith in the healing I was continuing to experience. Take a moment to think of a situation in your own life; it can be something very simple. Are you willing to see it differently? What is the lesson this experience could be attempting to teach you? The universe will continue to bring you a lesson until you learn it, until you move beyond it and graduate to the next thing, just like how you must pass one grade to get to the next in school. In hindsight, you may realize that somewhere you knew better, had a feeling (a knowing) that, if you took a certain action, took a step in a certain direction; things may not turn out the way you hoped. That voice, that feeling, is the voice of faith, the guidance from your power source of the soul. It is your GPS offering you a new way, steering you in a new direction. In hindsight, you can recognize where you listened and where you doubted. Those of little faith carry much doubt. Doubt is the energy of fear. Those who carry much faith carry much power.

My beliefs were changing: the belief that I was abandoned and unloved, the belief that I was always going to be in pain, and the belief that "shit happens." The more I consciously turned to faith, the more I let these beliefs be transformed. Beliefs cling to the old, faith lets go and allows new things to emerge. With faith, I am certain I am loved and loveable. With faith, I am certain that even in the difficult moments of my life, I am not alone. With faith, I am certain that my life has purpose. I realize my beliefs were based on my limited view and understanding of the universe and myself. Those beliefs were formed and acquired from others and not from a true understanding of the universe and the divine order of the universe. Beliefs contain limitation. Faith offers freedom from limitation!

> *"You don't have enough faith. I tell you the truth, if you had faith even as small as a mustard seed, you can say to this mountain, 'Move from here to there,' and it would move. Nothing would be impossible." Matthew 17:20*

A mustard seed of faith; just a small amount faith has the monumental power to move mountains. Are things progressing the way you would like in your life? If not, explore and contemplate this message. What could happen if you had faith in yourself? Can you have a mustard seed of faith in the guidance leading you in new ways? Your faith guides you toward a place where change is real; faith trusts in things that cannot yet be seen. Can you have faith in it, even if you don't believe it or see it yet? Faith is trusting in guidance, with no proof of the outcome. Uncommon faith is taking a risk. Uncommon faith will empower you to risk listening to this guidance and trying something new. The greatest of risks often bring the greatest of rewards.

Mike knew it was time to take his next step and risk trying something new. It was time to take a leap of faith. When I met Mike, he was nearing retirement from a lifelong career and had been dealing with some serious challenges in the form of health. His body was demanding attention and care. His soul called out for something new and guided him in new ways. The voice of faith encouraged and reinforced the fact that poor health was not where Mike was meant to stay. He had to choose to live in new ways and, in that, heal.

The beauty of watching someone heal is to witness purpose unfolding right before your eyes. Over the years I have been witness to the healing in Mike and how by healing, Mike's faith was reignited. He has retired from his career and has faithfully stepped up to the healer within his heart. He went back to school, studying massage therapy and reiki so he can share the gifts of healing with others. That is divine purpose in action!

Faith-filled testimonial

"I had been through some traumatic health issues that had left me very close to being on my death bed. I felt like I had two ways to go: die or heal myself. I'm a survivor, so I chose to find alternatives that would bring healing to my mind, body and soul. So choosing to live was the beginning of my journey. Faith was that unknown belief that I would actually find ways to make this happen! I started slow and deliberate. At a certain point, I knew I was ready to go to the next level. I was looking for something; I needed to find a teacher, but not just a teacher but somebody I would truly be connected to. I found Felicia and instantly knew she was the one. I could see straight into her heart and knew that was the heart I wanted. The healing and energy she brought to others was exactly what I wanted to share with others. I truly believe you are either being healed or you are healing others. That is my purpose. By faithfully following my inner guidance I was taken in the right direction."

Michael O.

To follow the pull of your heart in a new direction is the courage to do something new, to take a leap of faith into the unknown. The leap of faith is different and unique to each individual. For you this can mean making that first call for information from the school you dream of attending. It can mean showing up to your first yoga class and seeing what happens. It can mean having that conversation with a loved one that leads to reconciliation. It can mean, right here and now, opening up to the possibility of being happy and hopeful for something new to appear in your life. With just a mustard seed of faith, you can move mountains and overcome any obstacle!

Joshua had this kind of faith; he was bold enough to ask with a degree of faith so uncommon that the sun stopped in in the sky and allowed him to defeat his enemy. Others would say that is impossible. *"I don't believe the sun could be stopped in the sky. I don't believe that my life can or will change. I don't believe I can trust people again. I don't believe I am loveable or worthy of love. I don't believe in myself."*

With faith, all things are possible. Letting go of limited beliefs releases the power of faith to go work in your life. You release the power of uncommon faith by taking action. You release the power of uncommon faith by being bold enough to ask and have faith enough to trust.

Have a moment of faith, a mustard seed of faith, to challenge outdated and limited beliefs. Beliefs are things we are convinced of and things that may or may not be true. They are concepts and ideas that we gather from our past experiences and limited information. Allow your beliefs to change and let the past be the past. Believing in things that aren't true, believing in lies, completely hinders the full power of faith. Beliefs limit and can prevent an individual from seeing and believing in the miraculous. There are divine lessons and purpose inside each difficulty. Uncommon faith dares to know and understand this. Faith miraculously transforms the difficulty into divine purpose. Faith allows for new and miraculous things to happen in your life. Faith is the miracle power that can move the mountain from here to there. Faith is the miracle power that stops the sun in the sky. Faith is the miraculous power of the divine that is a part of you and is within you. Change your beliefs and invest in faith. Beliefs are limiting; faith has unlimited power. Faith unleashes the superpower of the heavens right where you stand. It is the power of Joshua to be bold enough and have enough faith that the sun stops in the sky. This power is what is required for you to live in alignment with your destiny!

*Have faith in the possibility of the new and
be bold enough to ask for things that seem
impossible; it allows you to take action in ways
you never thought possible.*

FAITH IN SOMETHING NEW

∽ Apply the Lesson
GETTING IN TOUCH
WITH THE POWER OF FAITH

Meditation:

Find yourself in a comfortable environment, somewhere with minimum distractions so that you can be undisturbed for a period of time. Sit comfortably either on the floor or in chair. If you are seated on the floor, have blankets or pillows under your bottom for support. If you are seated in a chair, either gather the legs under you or have the feet firmly planted upon the ground.

Sit with the spine straight, attentive to your posture. Let your eyes softly close and take a few moments to become quiet and attentive to the breath.

Continue in this manner for 5 to 10 minutes.

Contemplate:

⚙ What is your bold declaration of faith, the vision for your future, the dream you want to see come into reality?

⚙ Who limits me from bringing this dream to life?

⚙ What limits me from bringing this dream to life?

⚙ What do I believe stands in my way?

Notice the thoughts, things, people, sensations or emotions that arise in your mind and body as you contemplate these questions. Just be aware, simply observe.

Continue in this manner for 5 to 10 minutes

Take a deep breath in and hold it inside for the count of three. Exhale and release the breath fully. Repeat three times.

With faith all things are possible. ∽

Return to these questions:

- Who limits me from bringing this dream to life?
- Quietly inside state: "No one limits me; with faith all things are possible"
- What limits me from bringing this dream to life?
- Quietly inside state: "Nothing limits me; with faith all things are possible."
- What do I believe stands in my way?
- Quietly inside state: "Nothing stands in my way; with faith all things are possible."

On your next inhale, quietly inside begin to repeat the phrase:

- "With faith, all things are possible."

Simply breathe and repeat this faith-filled statement.

Contemplate all things being possible. Your vision is possible; your dream can come into reality.

Continue in this manner for up to 5 to 10 minutes.

When you are ready, take a deep breath and gently allow your eyes to open. Take out your journal and write down your responses:

- Who limits me?
- What are the limiting beliefs that I hold about myself?
- What limits me from bringing this dream to life?

Now, under each section, write and declare the following faith-filled answers!

- Who limits me? No one limits me; with faith all things are possible.
- What limits me? Nothing limits me; with faith all things are possible.
- What stands in my way? Nothing stands in my way; with faith all things are possible.

CHAPTER 8

Faith in yourself

*"Each experience in your life was absolutely necessary
in order to have gotten you to the next place, and the
next place, up to this very moment." Wayne Dyer*

Every experience in your life has brought you to
this moment, and the beautiful thing is that you
have survived. You can have faith in that. Life itself brings challenges, but faith knows these challenges are
necessary to develop your character and lead you step by
step to living on purpose. Life can be difficult when you
are disconnected from the true you and the true purpose
of your life. Everyone experiences moments of feeling
lost; lost in despair, lost in anger, lost in fear, sometimes
just plain *lost*. To live in a state of disconnection is to live
lost. Feeling lost, stuck and alone is at the core of living in
a state of struggle. Without faith, life loses its luster. You
may feel like you are moving aimlessly in life, focused in
the wrong direction, maybe working to change the world
and outside circumstances to make things right. There is
guidance; the voice of faith is always there reminding you
that you are not alone, that you are loved and supported.
Faith encourages you in all moments. The voice of faith
may have guided you to this book. The voice of faith has
guided me throughout my life toward people and experiences, even when I did not know it.

*I met Lisa in a small metaphysical store in our community,
we were attending a class on energy healing. As I sat near Lisa,
I sensed her warmth and Southern charm, but just under that I
could sense pain and frustration. Lisa is a true Southern girl, full*

of spunk and charm. She is one of those friends who will be at your door with a casserole at the first sign of trouble. She is willing to help in any way she can. As the day went on, everything in me wanted to reach out to her. A little voice inside me kept saying, "Tell her what you do. You can help her." Before I left that day I had a brief conversation with Lisa and told her to come and see me.

I was thrilled that she followed up and contacted me immediately. When Lisa came in she explained her conditions to me. She was struggling with diabetes, one step away from insulin injections; she needed to quit smoking, and was having regular migraines and periodic depression. She said, "I'm a mess." in her sweet Southern drawl. We began to talk about her life in general. I wanted to get a good picture of where she was with it all. In my work, I focus on the whole individual, not just their physical struggles but also what are the conditions of their life? What are the stresses? What is working and what is not? I counseled Lisa on the way she was seeing things. She had lost sight of the fact that there was a beautiful well-being inside of her. She had lost faith that things were going to change or that they could. I believe she came to me to figure out how to manage her physical health and life circumstance. Little did she know, that is not the intention of true healing.

I guided her to aspire for more, to have faith that something more than managing conditions was possible. She took a risk and had faith that this may be possible. I encouraged her step by step to ask for something more for herself. If she wanted to be in good health, have faith that good health is possible. If she wanted to be free of depression, have faith that happiness is possible. If she wanted to be free of migraines, have faith that when she shifted her view of her life the pain would end. Yes, she was not where she wanted to be, but celebrate that! It meant her voice of faith was guiding her to the next step. With faith, know that living in struggle is NOT your life purpose. Faith knows where you are is not where you are meant to be. You are meant to live a life of well-being and happiness. Lisa courageously took responsibility for her life and her life and made important changes from the inside out. I am happy to call "Ms. Lisa" a friend as well as a student.

FAITH IN YOURSELF

Faith-filled testimonial

"When I first met Felicia, I was searching for something, but I didn't know what. I had health issues, some of which were depression and smoking. With her honest yet loving help and healing, I have quit both. I had been on antidepressants off and on for 15 to 18 years and never off for more than a year. I have been off them for close to two years. After 29 years of smoking, I quit and have had no urge to start back, regardless of what goes on. I can be around smokers and have no urge. I credit this to my healing work with Felicia.

This year, I had some health issues and with her help I bypassed all healing expectations. She has taught me, through example, how it is possible to find the peace inside we all search for. She has taught about faith: We all fall, but getting up and moving forward will get us the results we are searching for. She shares her love, honesty, healing and intuition with us in the most loving and honest way I have ever experienced.

She has showed me that having faith works. It may not be what I wanted, but it was what I needed. I am learning to have faith in myself. I am learning that we all fall but the key is to keep getting up, brush yourself off, and consider, what did I learn from this? Then comes the "ah-ha!" moment. Falling was what I needed so I am stronger and more positive when I get up. Meeting Felicia has been, and still is, a beautiful journey of learning, love and understanding. She has taught me that we are always working on ourselves and we do not have to be perfect to help others, that our imperfections are beautiful and that these imperfections may be exactly what we need to move forward in our journey. Meeting Felicia has been the most positive and motivating thing that has ever happened to me. I am forever changed and faith-filled through our work together."

Lisa D.

With faith all things are possible.

The voice of faith is always there; do you dare to listen? Dare to be courageous enough to act and reveal the power of uncommon faith, the faith of action. Just a mustard seed of faith can move mountains and overcome any obstacle. In order to release struggle, to heal and to make monumental leaps of faith toward the future, it is necessary to acknowledge where you are, how you feel and what direction you are facing. This tells you which direction you are moving. Are you facing the future or looking to the past? To change your perspective of the past and to change your perspective of yourself is a powerful and courageous thing to do. It empowers you and switches your GPS back online. It is having faith, conviction and trust that there is guidance. It is challenging the limited beliefs of the past. This GPS system is guiding you up and out of the past. This GPS is guiding you toward love and divine purpose. What is keeping you from listening to this guidance? Are you facing the wrong direction? How can you move to your next destination if you keep going around the same block again and again? This block may be your past, this block may be your fears, and this block is what you have known for so long. It is the safe zone, the comfort zone. It may be difficult, but it is what you know. You don't know anywhere else to go. It is what you have known for so long that you may not even know that there is another way. There are other optional paths to take.

Uncommon faith knows how powerful you are. Each moment, each choice in life, is a choice whether to rise up to the light or descend into the darkness. A person of uncommon faith chooses, in all of life, to share light with everyone and in every experience chooses to rise to the light. In the most challenging times, choose faith over fear, light over dark. To choose the light of faith allows each situation to be transformed and utilized to teach in a way that guides you to your divine purpose. To choose faith is to heal at any moment in our life.

FAITH IN YOURSELF

Make a choice not to allow one person, one situation, one experience from the past define you and define your future. Your kindness, your love, your generosity and your trusting nature are the beauty and grace of you. Connect faithfully to these virtues. When you do, you let each person and each situation enrich you and uplift you. That is the true purpose that they are meant to serve. Have faith in a universe that is for you and wants you to succeed; it needs you to succeed. For when you succeed, you live in alignment with your divine purpose and destiny, and this serves the whole of humanity. Living in alignment with this divine purpose and destiny not only affects your life; it affects the destiny of the planet. When one is uplifted and healed, many others are uplifted and healed!

Use each experience as a means of learning. Then you are able to gather the wisdom contained within each thing, the miracle contained within each experience. Faithfully heal, faithfully connect and faithfully return to the beauty of your true self. When you return to this beauty, you release all things that are not in alignment with your destiny. You release all the people, situations, misconceptions and limited beliefs that weigh you down and hold you back.

It is time to take inventory of things, to commit to change. Disconnection from the power and guidance of faith shows up in life in the forms of depression, sickness, boredom, apathy, lack of passion, lack of direction, anger and, above all, *fear.* When you are living in connection with the guiding power of the soul, your GPS, it leads you to happiness, love, compassion, forgiveness, well-being and, above all, *faith.* Uncommon faith is sure that what is hoped for is possible, even though it is not yet seen. Ask the tough questions, without judgment:

- Are you happy where you are?

- Are you enjoying your life and work?

- Are you feeling love and connection?

Stand on new ground, stand firm in faith, and be courageous and strong enough to ask these questions. Be committed, disciplined and courageous enough to stop blaming the world and others for where you stand now. This is what it means to take the earth walk of uncommon faith. You take back your power when you stop blaming others and being a victim of the past. To take action is the power of faith unfolding in your life right here, right now. It is a choice to no longer be confined and defined by the past. When you take action, the level of uncommon faith is monumental and changes things for you in amazing and unforeseen ways.

I healed from my past, first by having faith that I could. In faith, I allowed myself to learn from the past and heal. I learned that the past contained miracles as well as difficulty. I learned that the past had taught me about the compassion in my heart. The healing process removed the blocks to my heart, and compassion is one of the virtues of the heart and soul. Compassion is the superpower of my heart and soul. Having faith connects you to a knowing about the purpose of things, for faith is wisdom. When you are connected to faith, you are connected to a vast power in the universe, the source of light, the source of faith. Faith has the miraculous power to transform things at any moment. Faith enables you to trust in this power. Trust in the guiding power of the soul; you are fully connected to it.

When I decided to stand on a new ground, a new energy entered my life; wisdom began to flow. This wisdom guided me to choose love over anger. This wisdom guided me to stop blaming the past and become responsible for my life. This wisdom guided me to look around and acknowledge what was working its way *into* my life and allow it. This wisdom, this inner voice of faith, guided me to take a risk, take a leap of faith. This wisdom assured me and I had conviction that my life would change in amazing ways. When I look back now, I can see these amazing changes. I have a life full of love, and

FAITH IN YOURSELF

my work in the world is sharing what I have learned and sharing what I love. Growing up, I had no real dreams; I just survived. Now my dreams are unfolding around me. For this to happen, I first had to take a leap of faith – to open myself to heal, to turn my gaze to the future and to walk forward in faith.

Faith is not blind to the truth of what the past has been; faith is visionary. Faith expands our limited view into broader possibilities. It is moving toward the vision of what you hope for but cannot yet see. It is to have conviction and trust in something before you can tangibly see it. It is trusting that the universe has a perfect order and knows what it is doing. To trust in the force that moves and holds this universe together perfectly and completely is a level of uncommon faith. Let our life be directed by a new power, the same power that makes flowers grow, keeps the planets in orbit and brings a child into the world. This same power brought you into the world. Faith opened me beyond my limited views and I now understand the universe is working for me, not against me, and each experience is essential and beneficial in my evolution.

Standing on new ground is activating faith. It is going from concept to conception. Invest your energy wisely. Faith in an idea commits energy to that idea. Do you have faith in your fear or faith in the divine? Where are you investing your energy? Invest your energy in faith by following guidance, the guidance that has you reading these pages, investing your time in reading these pages, and the message you are receiving from them. Invest in yourself, have faith in the guidance you are receiving, or at least be open to receiving guidance. Oftentimes guidance is sought, but when it is received it is left unacknowledged or disregarded, continuing to invest energy in fear. Fear is the energy of feeling small, contracted and powerless. Fear makes things feel impossible. Fear is a belief that makes us feel that we are unable to follow that guidance, the guidance of faith.

With faith all things are possible. ☙

This is the place where faith is miraculously powerful, to help you move boldly beyond belief and empower yourself to be able and willing to follow it! Uncommon faith is investing your energy in what is to come, rather than what has been. Uncommon faith trusts in what may seem impossible according to your beliefs. Move past limited, fear-based beliefs; each time you do, you will be transformed and empowered. The stumbling blocks, the difficult experiences, are then transformed into the stepping stones. Uncommon faith knows these experiences were not meant to defeat you, not meant to knock you down, but ultimately to lift you up. Uncommon faith knows these experiences are meant to teach you and develop the supernatural power, the divine power, within you. Uncommon faith transformed my past into my superpowers of compassion, forgiveness and love.

Beliefs have a preconception about the way things should be or should have been. Belief says, "*I will believe it when I see it.*" Beliefs keep you stuck in your preconceptions. Invest in the energy of faith, and allow the power of faith to go to work in your life. Stand on the ground of faith. Uncommon faith is the willingness to stand open-hearted in the present moment. It is the willingness to release judgment and dare, even risk doing new things and seeing things in a new way. Uncommon faith is the willingness to stand on this new ground with no guarantee or proof about what will happen next or what the outcome will be. Uncommon faith can invoke the end of difficulty. It is when the tides shift.

What I met Krista, the tides were shifting. She had come to the realization that she was stuck, and she could no longer recognize the woman she saw in the mirror each day. Krista is a wise teacher, a healer, and someone you would never think of as hard or angry. In her own wisdom, she knew that something was just not right. She knew that the tides were shifting and change was required.

FAITH IN YOURSELF

I was honored to help her pull back the layers of deception, the layers of fear, so she could stand faithfully in her power and take charge of her life. It was time to look things squarely in the eyes and make changes. She was no longer willing to blame those around her for the unhappiness she felt. She was ready to take responsibility for her own happiness. A person of uncommon faith is willing to take responsibility for their life and willing to make the necessary changes to live a life of purpose and happiness. Krista is one such individual.

Faith-filled testimonial

"I had a mid-life spiritual awakening at age 40, at about the time I began doing yoga full time. My life was crumbling before my eyes with thunder and lightning. There was nothing gentle about it; it was huge, powerful, scary and yet so very, very right. I had been a soul seeker for as long as I could remember, always wondering why we were here, feeling like it was do something big. But my heavily cloaked fear and doubt were in charge. So I became a hard-ass. I figured the harder I pushed and the more aggressive I was, the less likely it was that I would get hurt and fall apart.

Work with Felicia kept me from drowning. Time and time again she would throw me the life raft and I would hang on. I was a tough nut to crack, but she knew just how much I could handle and when. I remember the exact day she completely shifted my thinking from "I can't be married anymore" to a strong inner faith that "I am destroying my own marriage and taking him down with me." My husband expected me to come home and announce that I was leaving, and I came home and said, "I'm so sorry."

I am now a spiritual healer myself, and eternally grateful that Felicia was my guardian angel during those early years of awakening. Her faith in me, her guidance and her immense love are forever in my heart."

Krista S.

Uncommon faith is the willingness to act in boldness, to follow your guidance, and to trust in yourself and your life in an empowering way. It is the willingness to dig deeper and take responsibility for the life you are leading currently. It is being willing to change long-held beliefs and wake up to the purpose of your life and the circumstances you find yourself in. Uncommon faith knows each experience, each person, each place, is valuable and is teaching an individual miraculous and divine things. Stand in the midst of what you are resisting and, instead of letting your judgments, doubts, fears or ego take over, put your heart and energy into faith. Faith will make a way where there seems to be no way. Through faith, develop the qualities of strength, trust, patience, compassion, courage and love. Uncommon faith transforms each difficultly into a great asset and a great teacher.

Faith is the currency of the heavens: What you invest in, you receive a return from. When you take the step to stand on new ground, you activate the power of faith. Uncommon faith is the faith of action. Don't just think about faith, act on it! Acting on it activates this energy at a new level, the level of divine, supernatural strength. Uncommon faith risks and moves beyond limited beliefs, doubts and fears. Uncommon faith has no limitation. Beliefs can be limited and based on fear. Beliefs come from the ego, and the ego tends to:

Edge Guidance Out

What do you believe about yourself? Is it true? Make decisions from a place of faith and it leads you to freedom. Make decisions based on fear and it leads you toward more struggle and limitation. Faith says, "Yes, *have the baby when the time doesn't logically seem right.*" Faith says, "*Yes, quit your job and go back to school.*" Faith says, "*Yes, leave this relationship and choose loving yourself.*" Faith says, "*Yes you can. You are more powerful than you know; you are a divine spiritual being capable of amazing things.*" Be bold enough to have faith in what you may not be experiencing just yet. Sometimes you just have to fake it until you make it. Affirm the possibility of what the voice of faith is offering you. Have faith that you have divine pur-

With faith all things are possible. ᏀᏇ

pose. Have faith that, within you, you know the truth. Have faith in the light you carry.

Have faith in your ability to live in the light. Have faith in your ability to be a shining example of living a life of faith. Light is the place of wisdom. Light leads you away from darkness and ignorance. Light guides you home to truth and home to yourself, your true self. Have faith in your light and know it comes from the source of light that shines in all of us. You are not alone and never have been; spirit resides in faith. Spirit lacks ego and never chooses to edge out guidance. It stands open-hearted in the light of awareness, in the light of truth, and in the light of faith. Use this light, the light of faith, to lift yourself out of the darkness and transform yourself from within.

"You are the light of the world." Matthew 5:14

The beautiful thing about light is no matter how dark a place is, no matter how long darkness has prevailed, with one click of the light switch, light fills the space. No matter how long you have felt stuck, in pain and alone, one flick of the switch of faith and the light of faith floods in. Right now, flick the switch, challenge a belief and move beyond it. Have faith in your ability to do so. Faith is the currency of heaven, and it brings the wisdom of the heavens. Allow the power of faith to go to work in your life.

You can only begin where you are. Stop waiting for your destiny to land at your doorstep, and take action. Uncommon faith is taking action on the ground you are standing on right now. Transform your life by transforming each moment and each activity. Turn the ordinary into the extraordinary. Our divine purpose is not about the job we have or the roles we play; it is about the energy we bring to those things. If you will not invest in the power of faith where you are, you limit the power of faith to take you where you are meant to be.

- If your purpose is one of service, serve the one before you.

- If your purpose is one of inspiration, inspire the one before you.

- If your purpose is one of healing, heal the one before you.

- If your purpose is one of loving, love the one before you.

- If your purpose is one of compassion, be compassionate to the one before you.

Service, inspiration, healing and love are wrapped inside of divine purpose for us all. We are here to serve, inspire, heal and love.

Have faith, it is the currency of the heavens.
Invest in faith, and watch the power of the
universe unfold in your life!

∽ Apply the Lesson
GETTING IN TOUCH WITH ENERGY

Meditation:

Find yourself in a comfortable environment, somewhere with minimum distractions so that you can be undisturbed for a period of time. Sit comfortably either on the floor or in chair. If you are seated on the floor, have blankets or pillows under your bottom for support. If you are seated in a chair, either gather the legs under you or have the feet firmly planted upon the ground.

Sit with the spine straight, attentive to the posture. Let your eyes softly close and take a few moments to become quiet and attentive to your breathing. Let your hands rest comfortably on your lap. Simply feel the breath flow in and flow out. All your awareness resting on the rhythm of breath as it flows in and flows out.

Continue in this manner for 5 to 10 minutes.

As you breathe, let your mind begin to review the most recent day of your life. If you are doing this meditation in the morning, contemplate the prior day. If you are doing this meditation in the evening, contemplate the day just ended. From the space of the witness, the true "I Am," observe yourself going through this day, all the places you went, all the people you came into contact with, all the work you performed, all the experiences of that day.

See yourself arise in the morning and contemplate:

"Where did I go throughout my day?" See yourself prepare for your day. How did you begin your day? Who did you spend your morning with? When you left your home, where did you go? What did you do? Who did you spend time with? Where did you spend your lunchtime?

Contemplate all the places you invested yourself and your energy in throughout that day. Each person and each experience was an investment of your energy, your vital life force. Review the day and breathe.

※ Where did you invest your energy?

※ Who did you spend time with?

※ What places did you visit?

※ What activities did you participate in?

※ Simply breathe, contemplate and review your day.

Continue in this manner for 5 to 10 minutes.

Visualize yourself standing in the center of your day, with cords of connection extending out to each person and place that you invested your energy during that day.

Take a deep breath in and a deep breath out and state,

"I release myself from these experiences, people and places. I call my energy back to me."

Visualize those cords dissolving from each person, each place and each experience. As these cords are dissolved this allows all your energy to return back to you in the present moment.

Take three deep, cleansing exhales.

Inhaling through the nose and then exhale through the mouth, consciously let go.

Bring your attention to the base of the spine and visualize a ball of light; see this ball of light swirling at the base of the spine. As each breath comes in and goes out, the ball of light grows in strength, brilliance and power. The energy within you fills and revitalizes your entire body, mind and spirit.

Inhale and visualize this light extend upwards to the top of the head. Exhale and visualize this light extend back down to the base of the spine. Inhale your awareness; this light extends upwards to the top of the head. Exhale your awareness; this light extends back down to the base of your spine. Allow this breath, this light, this vital life force to clear and nourish you. Allow it to clear and nourish your body. Allow it to clear and nourish your mind. Allow it to clear and nourish your spirit.

Each day, consciously release the day before and align your energy to the present moment. As you go through your day, make a conscious choice of where you invest your time and energy.

When you are ready, take a deep breath and gently allow your eyes to open. Take out your journal and write down your responses:

⚙ Where do I invest my energy daily?

⚙ List the people and places that you invest time and energy into each day.

⚙ Do these activities or individuals nourish me or drain me?

⚙ Are these wise investments of my energy?

Be aware of where you put your time and energy daily. Today, invest wisely! Today, choose to allow each activity to fuel you; invest your time and energy wisely. Bring your strengths and your faith into each activity, each encounter and each moment. Each action and each activity becomes faith in action. Allow each of those activities to be a step toward your destiny.

CHAPTER 9

Faith in guidance

"Now faith is the substance of things hoped for, the evidence of things not seen." Hebrews 11:1

Uncommon faith dares to live in new and amazing ways. In the lowest moments of my life, the inner voice of faith emerged again and again. In those moments it came from the depths of my heart to lead me to the next place on my journey. It spoke to me and guided me out of harm's way and toward my destiny. Faith is innately within us ~ the mustard seed of faith planted in our hearts as we came into the world. In the moments we dare to open, dare to dream, it speaks. Faith is the substance of things hoped for, the evidence of things we cannot yet see. Faith allows us to dream big.

Will you be courageous enough to listen? Will you choose to act upon it? This is what a person of uncommon faith would do: not just think about change, but take action. Uncommon faith is the energy of action, taking the necessary steps to allow dreams and visions to come to life. Uncommon faith will move you dynamically in the direction of your dreams, toward the life you want, one step at a time. The key is that you must take the steps. Uncommon faith is to trust in those dreams even before you see them come to life.

"Faith is taking the first step even when you don't see the whole staircase." Martin Luther King

No matter where you are in life, there are choices to be made. Each day we make hundreds of choices. When you allow these choices to become conscious, you step up to your faith and empower yourself to create the kind of life you want to live. You open a space for the things you hope will manifest in your life. At the age of 28, I was searching, hoping and praying for change. I wanted something better for myself. I wanted to be free of pain. I wanted to be free of the past. Faith guided me gently in new directions. My life could only change when I took action, when I made new choices. I had to take action, step by step. Without action, nothing could change. I would remain where I was: in pain, unfulfilled and lost.

You may not know the final destination on your journey; who does? So focus here and now and choose to take a first step. As a baby, there is a moment when you decide, "If I want to get from here to there, I must learn to walk." Learning to walk is one foot in front of the other, one step at a time. Sometimes you fall, it is the way of learning, but you get right back up and begin again. Uncommon faith will direct your steps, one step at a time, toward something great. Each choice you make shapes the next moment. So if you want the next moment of your life to be different, choose something new. When you make conscious choices, you take responsibility for your life, how you feel and where you are. Responsibility means you no longer blames other, but instead ask, *What is my part? I may not be able to change the past, but I can choose to no longer be a victim to it.*

In order to change anything, action needs to happen. Empower yourself with faith and make new choices. You have a choice here and now. What you do here and now will determine and shape what is to come from this moment forward. To merely think about the changes you want to make is one thing, but unless you act, you will stay where you are. Action takes things from concept to conception. You can hope for things to get better, but you must have enough faith to act; this is the level of uncommon faith. It is beyond merely thinking of these changes. It is not only hearing someone mention a book to you, but buying the book and reading it. To not only hear about yoga, but to go to a class and get on the mat. Take faith-filled steps toward your dreams. Act on faith; act on the guidance you receive.

If your GPS system says go right, turn right! Empower yourself by following your own guidance.

While writing this book, I was struggling with completing this section.

I was on my way to my office and received guidance, a feeling that I should stop at the park and sit on the bench by the water. A part of me did not want to follow the guidance; the logical part of me said, "I don't have time for that today." I had been contemplating this book all morning. How could I relay the importance of listening to guidance? What was the direction this book needed in order to connect to others? These thoughts were swirling in my mind. I was experiencing a writer's block. I had been sitting in front of my computer for two days and nothing was happening. The words were forced. I asked for guidance and my answer was go to the park and sit on the bench by the water.

I made a choice to listen, just as I am asking you to do. I went that morning and sat and when I did the answers came. When I sat down, pad and pen in hand, I almost challenged this intuition by saying, "OK, I am here. What for?" I took a deep breath, looked at the water and just sat for a moment, just waited. Right then, the guidance I had asked for flowed easily and freely. I wrote this section and the final chapter. After that morning, the direction of this book unfolded and I was clear. Faithfully I chose to follow my GPS and turn into the park that morning. Faith will never let you down.

The Voice

There is a voice inside of you
that whispers all day long,
"I feel that this right for me,
I know that this is wrong for me."
No teacher, preacher, parent, friend
or wise man can decide
What's right for you — just listen to
the voice that speaks inside.
Shel Silverstein

With faith all things are possible. ෨

This voice knows what is right for you and what is wrong for you. No one can tell you what is right for you more clearly than you. Know that you are on your path. You may not like where you are on that path, but it is yours. On the path, if you don't do anything different and you don't act, you will stay stuck where you are. You can know meditation is meant to help calm your mind, but if you won't sit still even for a moment, how can it help you? You can receive guidance to go to church, but if you don't go, you won't get the message from the sermon. You can feel like you should eat better and exercise, but if you drive through McDonald's on the way to your couch, how will you begin to feel well?

Julie walked into my office, not sure of why she was there. She had no idea about the type of work that I did. She was stepping way out of her comfort zone. She was discouraged with her work, her family and herself. Julie is a lover of animals; she owns a pet store devoted to bringing natural health to animals and works with local animal rescue groups to find homes for the planet's furry friends. If Julie had her way, she would have endless resources and land to give love and shelter to every animal she meets. I love this part of her sprit, the compassion that flows so freely outward to animals and people. Yet when I met Julie this compassion was not flowing toward herself. She knew she had a "good life," so why was she so unhappy?

Her answer came in the response of, "Go see Felicia." She began to ask a new question and the response was new. The answers to these type of questions comes in many forms; our job is to recognize the response to our questions. To make the choice to step into my clinic and follow that guidance opened a door of possibility. Julie and I worked together to examine her life and get in touch with the compassion that flows so freely to furry and non-furry friends in a new way. In a way, that also supports her. At her core, Julie needed to have faith that she is worthy of compassion, she is worthy of happiness and she is right where she is meant to be. Julie was standing in the center of her life, living on purpose and not even realizing it! With faith, Julie came to see me and continues to do so. With faith, Julie knows she is doing what she is meant to do. She is an advocate for the furry friends of the world, she is a friend, she is a wife and she is happy.

Faith-filled testimonial

"Without question, the greatest gift I've given to myself was making the choice to walk into Felicia's clinic. I was in a very lost, confused and upsetting place in my life. With Felicia's guidance and faith-filled hard work, I now know that I deserve everything in my life. I have faith that I matter and I'm worthy of happiness. There are no excuses in Felicia's presence, just a whole lot of love. She has taught me that life is what you make of it. Make choices to surround yourself with positive energy and positive people and leave the rest behind. I am a different person today. For her energy, her love, her guidance and most importantly, for the work she has had me do to get me where I am today, I will forever be grateful. I have faith in myself."

Julie B.

What is the voice within you saying? When this voice speaks, it begins as a whisper, but the more you tune in, the more you listen, the more clearly you hear it. This voice speaks in the world in the form of repeated messages. What is the repeated message around you? What is the message or answer you receive each time you ask for assistance? When I was searching and praying for change, the repeated message was yoga. Everywhere I went yoga was mentioned, every bulletin board had classes listed, and when I would meet people, they would talk about the yoga class they had attended. Listening to this message was the way I tuned into the voice of faith. Faith is the connection to your soul. Listening to your voice of faith is listening to the divine force contained inside you, that is you. Tune into the voice of the soul, the voice of faith. The soul is above fear and doubt, and is the strength of you. It is the unbreakable aspect of you, the eternal you, the one that came here to grow and evolve, the part of you that knows who you truly are and what you are truly meant to do and be.

> *"We are not human beings having a spiritual journey. We are spiritual beings having a human journey."* Steven R. Covey

When I began to make different choices, such as attending yoga, meditating, refraining from acts of anger, reading different types of books, choosing to say yes when I always said no, my life took a turn in a new direction. I stopped merely thinking about change. I actively took steps in new directions. I listened to my own guidance, my intuition, the voice of faith. I had a good feeling about things, and I began to recognize that certain things just kept showing up before me. When I stopped focusing on what was wrong all the time and on what I was angry about, I allowed something new to come into my life. The stronger I began to feel, the more I had faith in myself. This strength gave me the confidence to follow my GPS. Faith empowered me to believe it before I see it and act like it is there before it is.

This seed of faith grew within me, strengthened by each choice and each step I took in a new direction. Uncommon faith developed and strengthened each time I trusted the guidance. Uncommon faith developed so I could dare to say *yes* to the new and the possibility of change, the possibility of healing. Uncommon faith is empowering yourself to heal.

Acting in the energy of faith changed my life because it changed me from within. It connected me to my inner GPS, and to a knowing that I was equipped me with everything I needed to overcome any difficulty I had experienced in my past. I found a courage that I could trust in and have faith in. I realized I had courage all along. This courage had moved me out of harm's way time and time again. This is the courage that arose in me at 4 years old and guided my family to leave my father. This is the courage that guided me to leave Kansas and my abusive husband. This is the courage that has me sharing my story in the form of this book. I have truly found my purpose. I now live in a new reality!

The purpose of this life, and its experiences, is not to make ourselves what we think we should be. The purpose of life, and its experiences, is to reveal who we truly are. You are a powerful, divine, beautiful and faith-filled being. Your soul did not come here to be comfortable, it came here to grow and learn. Character is developed in the difficult times. It is the way your strength, your patience, your courage, your compassion and your resilience are developed. Faith is a muscle that you develop through consistent use. Every time you empower yourself with faith, you invoke a divine power, a superpower of the universe. It is a power that moves mountains, defeats all enemies and transforms difficulty into divine purpose. This is the teaching of the mustard seed of faith. Faith is the mustard seed of greatness inside of you. When you stand in the great and divine power of your heart and soul, you can move mountains, you can overcome any challenge. You will rise out of the ashes of the past and emerge like a phoenix, more powerful than you may be able to comprehend. Faith does not exempt you from difficult times; it carries you through them with a grace of energy. Faith carries you through with a trust that you will come out on the other side of the challenge victorious, triumphant and stronger than you were before. Faith tells me this situation is not permanent; this is just a storm, and I am sheltered by my faith.

This level of uncommon faith is tested and passes the test. Faith doesn't magically increase on its own; it takes dedication, commitment and, above all, action! Faith becomes the place you turn to in order to make a decision. It is a place within you that you trust in to guide you and never lets you down. You trust in it during the challenging times and the good times. You trust it to lead

With faith all things are possible. ⟨◌⟩

you through the challenging times gracefully and with a knowing that it is taking you to the next step on your journey. When things become uncomfortable, it is a sign that growth is happening. This is the process; this is the evolution. When you rely on faith, trust in faith, you will be guided to new experiences, people and situations that will benefit you in ways you may or may not realize. This is how I end up working with people; they follow their guidance to me.

Angela reached out to me at a time in her life when she felt aimless. When I met her, I was taken with her beauty, not just her physical beauty, which is easy to see, but the beauty of her heart. Her heart had a calling, a desire, to help others. When I met her, she was just starting to receive this broadcast from the voice of her soul. Her life from the outside view was perfect, a life that many desire; a life of family, abundance and possibility. Yet Angela felt unfulfilled and unhappy. She needed to connect to purpose.

In our work, Angela grew ever more confident in what she had to offer others. She began to understand that her heart's desire and her divine purpose is to help others. As she grew more confident in this understanding, the question became: How? Once she got present, she was able to know how. In the now, you know how.

Faith-filled testimonial

"I began working with Felicia in 2008. At that time in my life, I felt very lost and wondered what I was put on this Earth to do. Over the years, there's really not one aspect of my life that hasn't been touched in some way from our work together. Of course, some questions remain, but through Felicia's guidance and the work, she has helped me realize that I was put here partly to serve. Shortly after a session with her, I was guided to participate in the Off the Mat Seva challenge, which allowed me to raise $20,000. Since then, I have continued on that journey of raising money for various local charities, through a golf classic that was established to help local charities. To date, we have raised over $51,000. I am so thankful that I have been guided to see the potential that lies within me, not only for the betterment of myself, but the world around me and my community."

Angela R.

Uncommon faith develops through the growth process. A process is a series of actions taken to get to a particular end. Uncommon faith is a process that evolves and grows as you take action. Just as a mustard seed evolves and grows, each action taken in faith activates and grows this mustard seed of faith in ever-expanding ways. Initially faith seems like an idea, a feeling of something intangible. As you dare to act, faith becomes something more tangible. Faith becomes the ground upon which you stand. Faith guides your decisions and your actions. It is like first going to the gym with the idea and inspiration of becoming healthy. In order to reach that level, you must keep returning and keep working out. As you continue to open yourself to the power of faith and act upon it, you will experience change. Through

With faith all things are possible.

experience, faith moves from a thought to something more substantial. Your faith becomes something true and trusted in. Faith brings understanding in your life; it brings the wisdom of growth. Faith brings the wisdom of transformation. Uncommon faith has the wisdom of experience at its core; it is a mature faith.

Faith, by its nature, must be tested. It is how faith matures and learning can happen. It is the way it increases. Each individual is exposed to the right experiences, people and situations to test, develop and empower them. This is the nature of how faith works. Through the tests, the trials of life, the dark times, an individual develops and matures like a seed in the dark. In the dark, the seed germinates, the outer shell breaks off and the plant sprouts a blossom. The blossom produces fruit and then flowers into its full beauty and potential. When our faith is tested and able to pass the test, our trust and confidence in the guidance and the support of the universe becomes a fact. There is no longer doubt about its power! Uncommon faith trusts and has confidence in your ability to overcome any difficulty and not just survive, but thrive.

A mustard seed grows and thrives because of the elements it encounters. A mustard seed is very small, but it grows into a very large plant, up to 9 feet tall! This seed of faith is in you, and when it is tested, it grows into a large and firmly rooted plant. When a mustard seed grows, it is a plant that takes over the land. It transforms the land into a land of mustard seeds. The mustard seed plant grows large enough to become a sanctuary for the birds and other creatures of the land. When this mustard seed grows within you, it becomes your sanctuary. When this mustard seed grows within you, faith takes over. Faith becomes the basis of your decisions. Faith becomes the eyes through which you see, the ears through which you hear, the power from which you do all things. And all things are possible in the energy of faith.

Faith is the answer "Yes" – yes to a way opening up, when the situation may not be showing you a way.

You want to attend school, but you don't know where the finances will come from? Yes combined with faith has the power to make a way and open the doors to the financial aid you need. You want to find love. Yes combined with faith has the power to bring love into your life. You want to open your own business. Yes combined with faith has the power to draw the right people and resources into your life. Yes combined with faith can carry you in a new direction.

So often the habit of *"No"* arises. There is fear of the unknown. No is easy to control; nothing new comes in and nothing old leaves. Yes opens the doors of your heart, and the heart is where faith resides. Faith resides in the spirit, which has an expansive view of things. Your spirit knows where you are meant to be and who you are meant to be. Take a daring step toward change and transform difficulty into divine purpose. Uncommon faith is bold enough to declare, *"Yes to change. Yes to opportunity. Yes to the unknown."* No is rejection. No rejects the opportunity, the person and the situation that is right before you. No creates sameness. Yes allows the impossible to become possible.

> *"What you resist persists, what you fight grows stronger. Always say yes to the present moment. What could be more futile, more insane, than to create inner resistance to what already is? What could be more insane than to oppose life itself, which is now and always now? Surrender to what is. Say YES to life and see how life suddenly starts working for you rather than against you."* Eckhart Tolle

Uncommon faith chooses to move past fear and be bold enough to answer "yes." Faith is the little voice in your heart that says yes when the world around you says no. Faith makes a way where there seems to be no way. Uncommon faith is bold enough to say yes and see where that leads you and what it leads you towards. Fear arises the closer we are to the truth. Right at the moment of breakthrough, fear will come up, but know the universe is a universe of balance. The counterpart of fear is faith. Choose faith; know there is another option. The option of faith is an option to say yes, even when, especially when, you don't have a guaranteed outcome. That is what faith is all about. Faith is the substance of things hoped for but not yet visible. What are you hoping for, praying for and wishing for? If you continue to say no, you may lose hope. Hopelessness is giving up, giving up dreams and giving in to fear. Can you receive if you say no? Uncommon faith is willing to receive. Each time you receive, it gives you trust and confidence in the power of faith. The mustard seed grows. What if, just for today, you said yes and watched what happened?

To say yes is to step into the unknown, and that is what faith is all about. It is about embracing life's experiences and challenges. Fear says no. No keeps things the same, keeps things under our control, and limits the vast power of the universe that wants to work in your life. Yoga came into my life and changed my life because I said yes. I was praying, hoping and wishing that things would change. I wanted out of the job I was in. I wanted out of pain and anger. I wanted to feel love. All these things became possible the day I opened up, had uncommon faith to declare, "My habit is to say no, but today I say yes!"

Having faith in the power of yes is having faith in the power of opening to the possibility of new and unexpected opportunities to unfold in your life, right here, right now!

FAITH IN GUIDANCE

⟶ Apply the Lesson
GETTING IN TOUCH WITH OPENNESS

Meditation:

Find yourself in a comfortable environment, somewhere with minimum distractions so that you can be undisturbed for a period of time. Sit comfortably either on the floor or in a chair. If you are seated on the floor have blankets or pillows under your bottom for support. If you are seated in a chair either gather the legs under you or have the feet firmly planted upon the ground.

Sit with the spine straight, attentive to your posture. Let your eyes softly close and take a few moments to become quiet and attentive to the breath. Rest your hands on your lap with the left palm facing up and the right palm facing down. Each breath bringing more ease and relaxation.

Simply follow the inflow and outflow of breath. Thoughts will come and thoughts will go; just stay with the simplicity of the breath, flowing in and flowing out.

On your next inhale, quietly inside state: "I am open."

On your next exhale, quietly inside state: "I let go."

This is the natural rhythm and wisdom contained inside of the breath. Not holding on to the breath that comes in, just "I am open." Not holding onto the breathe going out, just "I let go." This is the natural state of openness.

Inhale: "I am open."

Exhale: "I let go."

Continue in this manner for 5 to 10 minutes.

When you are ready, take a deep breath and gently allow your eyes to open. Take out your journal and write down your responses:

* What are you open to? Does it need to be defined before you will receive it?

* Am I comfortable when I receive?

* Do I accept help?

* Do I accept compliments?

Make today a day of yes. Start your day saying yes to the promise and possibility of the new day.

* When someone gives you a compliment, receive it!

* When someone offers you help, accept it!

* Whatever situation you find yourself in today, meet it fully open, without resistance.

Say yes to what the situation is bringing an opportunity for.
Say yes to your life.
Uncommon faith dares to say YES!

CHAPTER 10

Faith in yoga

"Yoga is a way of life, the uniting of the body, mind and spirit. Its real purpose is not just to become physically fit or mentally relaxed but also to deepen our own spirituality, enabling us to be more caring and aware, ultimately leading to self-realization." Judith Lasatar

The yogic path is rich and rewarding. It is an ancient practice that applies easily to modern day life, but dates back over 5,000 years. The word yoga comes from the Sanskrit language, the ancient language of India; its root is the verb yuj, which means "to unite." Yoga is the uniting of body, mind and spirit, the union of the material with the spiritual, the union of the seen and unseen aspects of ourselves. In unity there is wholeness. The Yoga Sutras are the handbook of yoga, as explained by the great teacher Pantajali. In the Yoga Sutras, the path of yoga is mapped out for practitioners. The Yoga Sutras explain the techniques of yoga that align the practitioner to the state of union. The Yoga Sutras cover all aspects of life, on and off the mat. The practice of yoga connects the practitioner to the divine being within and teaches how to bring that divine aspect out to touch the world. It is a tangible means of change; it is something you can practice as a means of transformation. The Yoga Sutras are the step-by-step guide to this transformation. The promise of yoga inspires the practitioner toward the great purpose of self-realization and, ultimately, freedom, or *samadhi*. To achieve wholeness is to be free. It is the understanding of how to live fully engaged in the world but also in deep connection to the spirit. The world needs and calls all of us to learn how to do this. To live life fully awake and aware is to end the cycle of disharmony and disconnection. Living in wholeness is living in harmony, peace and connection with ourselves and with one another.

Yoga taught me how to have faith in my body, faith that I wasn't meant to live in pain. Yoga taught me the transformative power of connection and self-realization. Yoga brought me home to my body in a grounded and powerful way. The practice chipped away at the pain within every cell of my body. Yoga brought me to the present moment through the power of awareness. The practice of yoga continually shows me where I stand and what direction I face in a real world sense. The yogic path was a giant leap of faith; in order to transform and heal from the pain I was carrying, first I had to practice. I had to faithfully show up on the mat and trust in the practice to heal and transform me without any proof of this outcome.

When I found yoga, it became the place I could rest and heal. It was a place where I could feel safe in my body. Yoga practice slowly started to unravel the years of tension and the pounds of stress I was carrying. Yoga practice became my sanctuary. In 2000, I attended my first yoga class at a local fitness center. This class initiated a change from deep inside of me; something shifted from the inside out. I did not understand how, what or why. I walked out of class free from pain and with an unfamiliar quietness in my mind. I knew that I wanted and needed to come back to my mat again and again. The practice watered the seed of faith inside of my heart. My heart knew and had faith in the fact that it was possible to get better and feel better. This was a monumental moment of awakening for me! Nothing in my life had changed just yet, but I sensed it could. It brought me peace to just know where my feet were planted. One of the most profound things I've found about the practice of yoga is that it brings you into the present moment, into your body, in a way you may have not experienced before ~, to simplify things, down to the level of standing on the mat, feet planted, heart open and mind attentive to the small details.

When I stood on my mat, I put aside the thoughts in my mind. When I did that, I also put aside a level of pain I was living in. I began to understand that much of what I thought was physical pain was actually mental and emotional pain. Until I encountered yoga, I had not put this together. I had searched far and wide for answers and solutions to the physical pain, but I was searching outside of myself. Yoga is a journey of discovery: the discovery of you. Yoga on the mat is one of the most tangible places to start this journey of discovery.

The voice of faith guided me to the mat, the place where I could let go of pain and chaos. The voice of faith came repetitively; everywhere I looked for answers, the word yoga arose. Thankfully, I had the wisdom to show up on my mat and follow that guidance. The yoga practice initiated moments of clarity, for it calmed the chaos. The yoga postures taught me how to be in the now. Every time I faithfully returned and continued to return to my mat, my life improved and my health improved. Yoga taught me to identify with the spirit of me. I could see the world clearly through the eyes of presence and peace. I am better in all ways because of my faith in the power of yoga.

I began to seek out a teacher of yoga. I wanted to learn more and needed to understand what I was experiencing and why. It is said that when the student is ready, the teacher will appear. This is a true statement for me. I met Laura Tyree, owner of Dragonfly Yoga in Fort Walton Beach, Florida. She was teaching at a local community center, just having moved to Florida. I walked into class a few minutes late, not knowing this was bad etiquette. I unrolled my mat with a snap and joined the rest the class already in practice. I took the posture downward dog, and I was home. I remember Laura coming by and saying to me that this was a closed session. I did not respond, but I thought inside, "I am not leaving. Please don't make me go."

It was as if she heard me; she let me stay. I finished the class and returned in a few days. She approached me and mentioned that she was opening a studio and would be starting a teacher-training program, and asked if I was interested. My knee-jerk response was to say no. So, not knowing why she asked me this, just out of habit I said no.

When I left that night, I heard the inner voice again. It would not let this conversation go. It was the voice of faith. It was the GPS saying, "You have arrived at your destination." This was so true; I was in a job that was making me increasingly unhappy. I wanted to change. I was exploring things that would allow for change. I was, for the first time in a long time, starting to know moments without physical pain. I was being shown signs of possibility. I was being shown opportunity in the form of a new relationship, new friends and yoga.

Within a day or so I called Laura and said, "My habit is to say no to new things, so I'm going to change that habit now and say yes to this program, say yes to something different." This yes was one of the most profound decisions in my life, to stand upon my yoga mat and to say, "Here I am." Having enough strength and courage to say that to myself, and being willing to see who I was, was phenomenal considering the state I was in.

I began to connect me to my life and myself in new and profound ways. I started looking at the whole of my life and the whole of myself. This view was liberating and eye-opening. I realized my struggles were in large part due to the fact that I was living my life in pieces. My body was one piece of the puzzle, my mind another, my past another, and so on. I needed something to bring it all together. Yoga united the pieces of my life and myself by re-uniting my body, mind and soul. I had pieces of myself scattered all around me, I needed to put the puzzle pieces together. When I began yoga, I knew nothing of the soul. I did not know it in a book-learned way, in a philosophical way or any way I was conscious of. The practice of yoga woke up the soul of me. The more I practiced, the better I felt. I see this with my students who step onto the mat unaware, uninspired and without direction. When I begin classes now, as a teacher, I just ask them to stand and look at their feet. I ask them to see what direction their feet are facing, and from the ground up, align themselves to the present moment. In the present moment is the presence of the soul.

Atha Yoga anushasanama : Yoga Sutra 1:1
"With prayers for divine blessings, now
begins the sacred practice of yoga."
(Light on the Yoga Sutras: BKS Iyengar)

The state of union, the experience of yoga, can only be found and occur in the present moment, the place where everything is connected. The first Yoga Sutra uses a profound and powerful word, Atha, which means "now." Now begins the sacred practice of yoga. For me this now, this practice of yoga, has become the knowing of where I am and the ability to arrive fully in the present moment. In the present moment, I am not the past. I am not the pain of the past. In the now, I am free. I am free when I get in touch with the divine being inside of my heart, the "I am." This divine one is eternally free and is easily accessed in the present moment. Much like the breath, you cannot breathe for yesterday, you cannot breathe for tomorrow, you can only breath in the now. You access the "I am" every time you breathe in and breathe out in a state of awareness. Yoga teaches me and reminds me that I am a divine spiritual being inside a physical body. Every conscious breath is a deep connection to the now; every breath is a moment of freedom. The physical body is the temple of the soul. As I took greater care of the temple of my body, my soul was expressed fully, and in that, I have come to know who I truly am.

This is one of the most beautiful experiences that yoga has to offer. Anyone who practices yoga can become self-realized. This powerful practice connects you to the true you, the "I am" that is not all the past experiences, the "I am" that is wise and empowered. Yoga teaches that faith, or sraddha, is the means to wholeness. Wholeness is preceded by faith, dedication and sincere practice. Those who embark on the journey of yoga are empowered to have faith in their abilities and trust in the transformation that is occurring. Yoga connects the practitioner to the source of faith, the divine being within each individual. Yoga gave me faith in my body to heal, faith that my mind could calm, and faith that I was more than my body and mind. My faith increases and enlarges each time I step onto my mat and leave feeling stronger, calmer and in a state of connection and peace. In order to receive the benefits of the practice, you must faithfully show up. Have faith in yourself, which honors the divine within, and then simply practice. Each time you practice, power is unleashed within you.

Yoga is a magical formula: present moment = freedom

Yoga on the mat changes you not only on the mat, but also in your entire life. Remember, yoga is about bringing things together on all levels. Yoga gave me confidence in my body. As I felt stronger in my body, I felt stronger and clearer in all aspects of my life. I felt stronger than the pain and stronger than the depression. Yoga put me in touch with the strength of my spirit, which is light and amazing. Through the faith-filled eyes of your spirit, look at things with wonderment and a sense of innocence. In the present moment, judgment and expectation are released. Faith trusts in the raw experience of what is happening now. Living in a state of disconnection, misalignment and ignorance of who we truly are makes it hard to listen and connect to guidance, the voice of faith. It is like a radio station transmitting a broadcast you are not tuned into. The solution to the problem of how is simply connection. Simply and faithfully show up, and yoga practice will connect your body, mind and spirit to what it is designed to do.

Yoga brought me to the present moment in a way I had not experienced before. Yoga brings you to the raw experience of you on the mat. You meet yourself just as you are and work from there. You meet yourself in the present moment, the now. Now we begin the practice of yoga. In this kind of existence, an individual can let go of what they have known and what they think will happen, and trust. The first Yoga Sutra simply states, *"Maybe you have tried other things, but now you commit and step up to the practice of yoga."* Yoga is to stand in the present moment, receptive and expansive, able to question and learn from each experience in life. It is the choice to be here now and live in wholeness and unity. When you feel whole and without conflict, you are free to make wise decisions. You develop faith in the wisdom within your body, mind and spirit. Faith is an energy that is grown like a muscle. The muscle of faith must be exercised to be developed, just as the physical muscles develop through practice. Yoga emphasizes the importance of practice and dedicated effort.

There are times on the mat that things can shift in profound ways. Add the right mix of postures, breath and focused attention/intention and transformation is inevitable. In the fall of 2004, one such practice occurred. I found myself in a quaint studio in Mississippi where I had moved and joined the team as a teacher. This beautiful little studio became the place I found my voice as teacher and the place where I practiced yoga and deepened my dedication and efforts of creating balance and wholeness in my life.

We were nearing the end of the workshop and the session was winding down, I found myself in a safe and comfortable child's pose. I was there, simply breathing and reflecting on the intention of the practice. The teacher had opened the dialogue earlier with the question and intention of discovering: "What did we individually desire from the practice of yoga?"

As I contemplated the intention of my own practice, the teacher spoke about the role of desire and intention on the mat and in life. In that moment, as if for the first time I asked quietly inside, "What do I want? What is my deepest desire?"

I was surprised that no answer came up. I knew yoga was about self-realization, ultimately the connection and reconnection to the spirit of the practitioner. Yet somehow, I had not taken that theory into practice. Yoga was a means to relieve myself from physical pain and the chaos of my mind. Now I found myself ready to ask for more. This teacher brought up the point that if we didn't know what we wanted, how would we know we received it?

The next day I sat in meditation and contemplated the questions, "What do I desire and what do I want from my yoga practice?" The answer was surprising, the response was silence. The kind of silence that is not lacking anything but the kind of silence that is robust, alive and illuminating. I realized I sought to know the one at the core of my being. I truly desired to connect to the divine one inside me where I felt peace, freedom and wisdom. From that day forward yoga took on a new and more personal meaning for me. Now I know that my practice is teaching me about how to get in connection with the "I Am," the soul of me. The one within me, which is faith-filled and powerful. My deepest desire and intention was to know myself. To know the self that lives in the present moment and is free from fear, doubt and pain. With faith, I deepened my practice and realized I was actually receiving what I truly desired.

Each time you practice yoga, it deepens your faith in the power of this practice. Have faith in the ability of the practice to facilitate self-transformation ~ faith so strong that you will remain dedicated to the practice when things are difficult, boring or demanding. When you feel stronger in your body, you develop faith in your body. When you feel stronger and sound of mind, you develop faith in the power of a disciplined and focused mind. When you feel the quiet of your spirit pervading your everyday existence, you develop faith in your spirit. Yoga is the experience of oneness. It is first oneness within you, and then it is the ultimate understanding of the oneness of the universe. Have faith in the power of yoga to connect you to all that is. Develop faith through the direct experience of yoga. With faith-filled dedication, commit to showing up, and be in the now.

When you dedicate your efforts in yoga, you may experience the many benefits of yoga:

- Stress relief and relaxation

- Calming of the mind

- Heightened mental and intuitive awareness

- Authentic happiness

- Inner peace

- Increased lung capacity

- Increased overall energy levels

- Improvement in quality of sleep

- Stimulation of the immune system

- Increased strength and physical conditioning

- Improved posture

- Hormonal balance

- Reduction and alleviation of pain

Freedom is only possible in the present moment ~ freedom from what was and freedom from what is to come. Know you are free to stand in awareness in the now moment of your life. Experience the power of the present moment. Being in the now is freedom from the past. The past only continues to be in the present moment when it is brought to the present moment. The past only repeats itself because it is projected onto the present moment. Be in the now. The soul is always present in the now. Guidance is clear and available in the now.

Having faith in the now activates now faith;
right here, right now, all things are possible!

With faith all things are possible. ⌒⌒

❧ *Apply the Lesson*
GETTING IN TOUCH WITH
THE PRESENT MOMENT

Meditation:

Find yourself in a comfortable environment, somewhere with minimum distractions so that you can be undisturbed for a period of time. Sit comfortably either on the floor or in a chair. If you are seated on the floor, have blankets or pillows under your bottom for support. If you are seated in a chair, either gather the legs under you or have the feet firmly planted upon the ground.

Sit with the spine straight, attentive to your posture. Let your eyes softly close and take a few moments to become quiet and attentive to the breath. Place your hands on your lap with the palms facing down. With each breath, become ever more present to the breath simply flowing in and simply flowing out.

Continue in this manner for 5 to 10 minutes.

On your next inhale, quietly inside state: "I am"

On your next exhale, quietly inside state: "here now."

Simply breathing and repeating,

Inhale: "I am"

Exhale: "here now."

Continue in this manner for up to 5 to 10 minutes. Simply breathe and be aware.

Contemplate:

❀ Where are you?

❀ Who's there with you?

❀ What are you feeling?

❀ What are you thinking?

❀ What are you doing there?

Simply breathe and be aware, attentive to the present moment.

Whenever you become distracted return to the breath:
Inhale: "I am"
Exhale: "here now."
This is Atha; this is now; be here now.

> **When you are ready, take a deep breath and gently allow your eyes to open. Take out your journal and write down your responses:**

- What did you notice when you became present?

- What did you notice about your external environment? What is happening around you?

- What did you notice about your internal environment? What is happening within you?

Commit to the practice of now. Each hour set a reminder on your watch or phone, a reminder to get present. Stop and pay attention. Experience the power of the present moment.

Inhale: "I am"
Exhale: "here now."

CHAPTER 11

Faith in reiki

"Reiki, simply put, is a Japanese technique for energy balancing that addresses the whole of an individual: body, mind and spirit." Felicia McQuaid

Reiki is the conscious movement of universal life force energy in order to create balance, harmony and well-being. It is pronounced "ray-key." Rei is translated as "universal" and Ki is translated as "life force." Ki is the life force energy that flows through everything alive in the universe. Reiki is a Japanese technique for natural healing; this energy stimulates and supports the body's own self-healing mechanisms, enabling the body to do what it does best, *heal*. When you are in a state of wholeness, you are in balance. Balance is well-being. Reiki energy has one main purpose: to bring you into balance. Reiki transforms the energy of life by transforming the energy within each individual. Receiving reiki is somewhat like filling a cup to overflowing. Reiki energy flows from the universe into the individual; when this happens, there is an overflow. Think of pouring fresh water into a container: As fresh water comes in, the old water overflows. Reiki overflows and releases the energy you carry that is not consciously being directed toward healing. Reiki energy guides your system toward higher vibrations, the vibrations of spirit. You cannot fill a full cup, as reiki energy is poured in; the energy that overflows is that which keeps an individual from balance, health and well-being.

Reiki taught me the power of self-healing and self-care. Reiki taught me to have faith in my own ability to heal, and to release the old. It offered me a tangible connection to an unlimited source of energy, one that was full of compassion and love like I had not known in my life before. The law of reiki is that in order to heal others, you must first heal yourself. My divine purpose is to be a healer; reiki brought me one step closer to realizing this purpose. I healed myself and, in the process, I learned that healing is possible. I learned how to transform my difficult experiences of my life into my superpower of understanding and compassion. The capacity to heal is within everyone, no matter what you have been through.

I was introduced to reiki during my yoga teacher training in 2002. The group was being taught the importance of healing and the role energy plays in healing. I felt an immediate attraction to reiki energy; I knew it was something important for me. After the weekend, I signed up for a private healing session.

I had no idea what to expect as I reclined onto the table for my session. During a session, the recipient lies down on a table, in a quiet environment, fully dressed. The practitioner either touches or practices reiki "hands off" over a body. The practitioner uses specific hand placements to balance and redirect the flow of vital life force, or ki. As the session went on, I sensed emotions and feelings in my heart. I felt warmth in the hands of this woman. It was warmth you can feel in the form of heat in the hands, but also warmth like a hug on a tough day. I weeped; grief, fear and deep sorrow flowed out of me and then suddenly I was at peace. A rush of calm moved through me and the tears stopped.

It was transformative and oh so revealing. After the session, the woman I was working with guided me to spend time alone and journal. I went to the beach and wrote for hours. Years of pain poured out on the pages as if she had opened my heart and my story came pouring out. As I wrote, I forgave those I wrote about. As I wrote, I realized I had more to forgive and that I needed to love myself again. This experience woke me up to the fact that pain is carried not only in my memories but in my heart and soul. This session opened a space for me to heal and know there was a safe place to do that.

With faith all things are possible. ⟲⟳

Reiki empowers and puts the power of healing quite literally into the hands of the practitioner. Reiki is not a passive path; it requires commitment from the practitioner to become aware of patterns and to consciously allow reiki energy to enter in and transform these energetic patterns. Reiki energy is source-level energy; it is pure and intelligent. Reiki connects a person to pure, unlimited and transformative power in the universe. You can heal yourself. You can heal your life by transforming the energy patterns within you.

Changing your vibration changes your life. Reiki consciously and directly connects you to source energy, the highest vibration in the universe. Reiki energy is the energy of love and compassion. Reiki is amazing in the way it connects to you to and allows this beautiful transformational energy to enter your system. It brings in a new energy, and when something new comes in, something old must be released to make room for it. Reiki opens you up to a divine energy that pours through every part of you. Your vibration is changed by this energy; how could it not be? Reiki is the direct experience of love. The experience of love awakens faith. Have faith in the love that fills the universe and wants to fill you. Faith is an energy that lifts you into a new vibration, one that is stronger than fear, doubt and pain.

Reiki allowed me to connect to an energy that was not coming from within me, but flowing through me. Reiki taught me to surrender. Reiki is not done from your head; reiki flows into and awakens your heart. Your heart is full of faith, love and compassion. Reiki raised my awareness about what I was carrying in my unconscious, what I was carrying in my energy centers ~ or chakras ~ and what I was carrying within the cells of my body. It lovingly guided me to these places and brought light to them in a powerful way. Reiki taught me about my life purpose of healing. I believe we all share this purpose, the purpose of healing ourselves so we can heal the world we live in. Reiki taught me how to become my own best healer. Reiki is the tool of transformation we are gifted when we step onto this path.

Reiki leads the practitioner to the experience of whole-ness. In order to experience wholeness you must be con-scious and aware of the energy of you and your life. The ki of reiki is conscious life force energy, the energy of light. This ki brings the light of awareness to the ruts or habit patterns within you that keep in you imbalanced. This light of awareness reveals the root issue of the imbalances. Reiki reveals by illuminating the things of the unconscious that may hold you back or lower your vibration. Only when we become conscious or know something do we have the power to change. The past is carried, not just in memories, but as a vibration. The experiences of life are contained within your energy and within your vibration. Things that are not healed become the underlying control system, silently directing thoughts, actions and reactions. This keeps an individual stuck in ruts, confined to habit. This is what will continue to attract the same type of people and experiences again and again.

Learning reiki made perfect sense to me. I was the sum energetic total of my life, my experiences and the effect these experiences had on me. I learned about the chakra system, the anatomy of the spirit. The chakra system contains seven primary energy centers from the top of the head to the tailbone. The chakra system is the energetic book of your life. Each chakra, or "wheel," of energy directs the flow of ki that relates to physical, mental, emotional and spiritual functions. The chakras are the places we receive, absorb and distribute life force energy. When my energy was focused on pain and anger, I experienced my life through that vibration. Awareness is empowering. Reiki taught me to focus on love, well-be-ing, healing, compassion and forgiveness. Reiki gave me faith in assistance, a tangible place of connection that assists in healing. Reiki moved me beyond my limited beliefs and experiences. Reiki gave me faith in Source and my connection to it.

Reiki teaches the practitioner to not just manage the outer layer of symptoms, which show up as illness, anxiety, depression and confusion, but to look deeper to the cause, to the place of origin and change from within. The body holds pain from the past and, if left unhealed, will often manifest as some type of imbalance. Reiki has the power and capacity to shine light on the core issues creating imbalance. When you have consciousness, you have power. Reiki is the direct way of bringing conscious and powerful energy into your system.

To know Jewel is to love Jewel. Jewel and our work together tested my faith on so many levels. She was guided to me step-by-step and when we met we knew it was no accident. Jewel had to be helped as she walked into my clinic the first time. Her body was wracked with pain and she had no physical strength left. It was difficult to for her to walk, impossible to cry, and hard to witness. She was diagnosed with Lyme disease. Up until that point, I had not worked with anyone with this illness, or in this kind of pain. Yet, the voice of faith within me knew I could help her. Working with her was outside my comfort zone. All that I was certain of was that I was meant to help her. I had faith in that. She had moved mountains to find me, she was so desperate for help.

My faith was tested again and again with Jewel. I never knew what would come up in our private work. The amount of pain she was in was difficult for me to see. The mother in me wanted to save her and lift her out of pain. Jewel and I both knew that even if we could not see the benefit of our work just yet, the benefit of the work still existed. This is what faith is all about, trusting in what you don't see just yet. This level of uncommon faith can move mountains and overcome any obstacle, including this obstacle of Lyme disease. The power of faith lifted us both out of fear and away from doubt.

Jewel is an inspiration to everyone who meets her. She exudes a beauty that is hard to describe, a beauty that valiantly rises out of the ashes of illness and struggle. Like the phoenix that rises from the ashes of destruction and difficulty with strength and power. She is that phoenix. Her sessions and personal work outside the sessions created a space to heal. After some time together we began to see the tangible results of our faith-filled work. She walked unassisted for the first time in a long time. She was able to cry, she was able to scream and yell and release anger, and she was able to express herself. She could finally express the beauty of who she truly is. She could finally express the light of her and express the love of her. In faith, I know that this illness has a divine purpose. Jewel faithfully heals. She inspires others to heal and shows the world the power of healing. She shows the world the power of having faith. She is the example of living a life where, with faith, all things are possible. I cannot wait to see how Jewel will change this world. I have faith that she does and will continue to do so.

Faith-filled testimonial

"If there is one thing I have learned, it is to always have faith. My healing process was one of great triumph and inconceivable transformation. When I began working with Felicia, I was overcome by a debilitating disease and on the verge of spiritual collapse. Throughout the journey, time and time again I found myself at the crossroads of old patterns and infinite potential. With the guidance of Felicia's gentle wisdom, I was able to step outside of old patterns and discover a new, higher version of myself. Learning how to rise above the anguish and thrive in wellness was something I had nearly given up hope on, but faith carried me through. Every step of the way, Felicia flawlessly embodied compassion. From the moment I realized I was free of disease, I found myself on an inherent path to my greatest dreams. The path has always been harbored within my spirit, but it wasn't until my work with Felicia that I was fully awakened to its aptitude. Each day I find myself further and further along this beautiful path to the destiny I have created for myself. The world is my own and I am here to heal it. Felicia awoke the true 'I' within me."

Jewel C.

The beauty of reiki is its simplicity of practice. It gently and easily calms the body, mind and spirit. It has been shown to reduce anxiety, lower pain levels, reduce stress, curb insomnia and, most importantly, bring feelings of rest and ease. Reiki can be practiced in two ways: as a client receiving reiki from a practitioner or as a practitioner giving themselves reiki. Reiki is easy to practice and learn. It can be learned by anyone of any age, any background and any gender. Reiki is an open pathway to all who seek wholeness and well-being.

Faith in reiki develops through experiences. With your energy in balance, you will feel relaxed, refreshed, focused, free from pain, calm and connected. Reiki is a path of self-empowerment. The amount of time and energy you invest in reiki is what you receive back. Reiki teaches its students and clients to have faith in the innate capacity within each of us to experience wholeness, balance and well-being. As you become more aware of the habits within you and that show up around you, you become empowered to change what is not serving you. You begin to change not only at the level of thought, but at the level of vibration. Changing your vibration changes your life.

As you allow more love and compassion to flow through you in the form of reiki, anger, despair, worry, confusion and illness are alleviated and released. Reiki gave me faith in my ability to heal and to be free of the past and pain. Healing comes from the heart; reiki flows into the heart and then from the heart to where it is most needed and most beneficial. Reiki is a particular strand of energy in the universe that aligns us, consciously, to source energy. We are all connected to source energy, and, therefore, we all can learn and practice reiki. There are so many potential benefits to the practice of reiki. Welcome in the possibility of healing balance, harmony and health.

BENEFITS OF REIKI:

- Creates deep relaxation and aids the body to release stress and tension

- Accelerates the body's self-healing abilities

- Aids in better sleep

- Reduces blood pressure

- Helps with acute (injuries) and chronic problems (asthma, eczema, headaches, etc.)

❋ Aids the breaking of addictions

❋ Helps relieve pain

❋ Relieves anxiety and assists in the healing of mental disorders such as bi-polarism and schizophrenia

❋ Removes energy blockages

❋ Assists the body in cleaning itself from toxins

❋ Reduces some of the side effects of drugs and helps the body to recover from drug therapy after surgery and chemotherapy

❋ Supports the immune system

❋ Increases vitality and postpones the aging process

❋ Raises the vibrational frequency of the body

❋ Helps spiritual growth and emotional clearing

Having faith in the power to heal
allows for miracles to take place.

Apply the Lesson
GETTING IN TOUCH WITH THE HEART

Meditation:

Find yourself in a comfortable environment, somewhere with minimum distractions so that you can be undisturbed for a period of time. Sit comfortably either on the floor or in a chair. If you are seated on the floor, have blankets or pillows under your bottom for support. If you are seated in a chair, either gather the legs under you or have the feet firmly planted upon the ground.

Sit with the spine straight, attentive to your posture. Let your eyes softly close and take a few moments to become quiet and attentive to the breath. Place your hands in front of your heart, with the palms touching. Gently tune into your heart and the breath flowing in and out of you.

With your focus on your heart, breathe in deeply. Feel each breath coming into contact with your true self, in the center of your beautiful heart.

Continue in this manner for 5 to 10 minutes.

As your attention rests in the space of your heart,

Contemplate: "What does my heart need in order to heal and fully open?"

Remain open to the feelings, emotions, sensations, thoughts, memories or images that come forth. Simply breathe, contemplate and observe. Listen to your heart; what is it asking for?

On your next inhale:

Invoke or call this energy into you. If your heart needs love, invoke the feeling of love and breathe it in!

✸ Breathe in love; Breathe out faith.

✸ Breathe in compassion; Breathe out faith.

✸ Breathe in peace; Breathe out faith.

✸ Breathe in hope; Breathe out faith.

With faith all things are possible.

- Breathe in understanding; Breathe out faith.

- Breathe in courage; Breathe out faith.

- With each breath receive, and with each breath heal.

Continue in this manner for 5 to 10 minutes.

When you are ready, take a deep breath and gently allow your eyes to open. Take out your journal and write down your responses:

- What does my heart need in order to heal?

- What does my heart need in order to open more fully?

- What did it feel like to be tuned into my heart?

CHAPTER 12

Faith in buddhism

*"We already have everything we need. There is no need
for self-improvement. All these trips we lay on ourselves
~ the heavy-duty fearing that we're bad and hoping that
we're good, identities that we so dearly cling to, the rage,
the jealously, and addictions of all kinds ~ never touch our
basic wealth. They are like clouds that temporarily block
the sun. But all the time our warmth and brilliance are
right there. This is who we really are. We are only one blink
of an eye from being fully awake."* Pema Chodran

In my desire to understand the world in a bigger context, I discovered Buddhism. The path of Buddhism, for me, is not about a religion, it is about understanding. Buddhism offers practical tools and guidelines for living. When you live in awareness and understand that liberation is possible, happiness becomes possible. Buddhism brings understanding. It offers a view of the world that that is pragmatic and practical and makes spiritual sense of things. The core teachings of Buddhism are found in the Four Noble Truths, that there is suffering and an end to suffering. Buddhism offers a deeper understanding of your relationship with the world. It teaches concepts of impermanence, the understanding that *"This too shall pass."*

The world and our lives are always in flux, always in states of evolution. Buddhism teaches how to relate to life and consciously evolve. Buddhism offers faith in the order of the universe. Buddhism offers teachings about how the universe works. Buddhism teaches an individual to understand that, fundamentally, they are good, fundamentally, they are compassionate and loving, fundamentally, they are forgiving and strong, and fundamentally, they are faith-filled and powerful. When Buddhism came into my life, it taught me to accept my divine nature as my true self and let go of the rest. Buddhism woke me up to the fact that I am fundamentally good, and that there is beauty, warmth and light within me. Buddhism woke me up to these facts. It was an amazing concept to suddenly think of myself as fundamentally good -- to realize the warmth and beauty that I experienced with reiki was me, it is my heart.

Buddhism says to look within and uncover the goodness of you that is clouded by the pain, disappointments and struggles. Pain is inevitable in life; every individual experiences challenges and has lessons to learn. Buddhism teaches about impermanence; the very nature of the universe is that things come and go. The First Noble Truth is that suffering comes from clinging to the things of the world that are impermanent. Pain is inevitable in life, but suffering is optional. Suffering in the context of Buddhism is feelings of dissatisfaction that take away the joy of living. Yes, I experienced pain in life, but I suffered because I brought it into the here and now. Suffering is carrying the old into the new. I suffered because I identified with the past as who I was. I identified with the clouds that blocked the light, not the light behind those clouds. The First Noble Truth is to understand that there is suffering in the world, there are difficulties that will be encountered, but also to understand -- as is laid out in the Four Noble Truths -- there is a way out of suffering. There is an evolutionary process of change.

There is beauty within you. No matter what you have been through, there is a diamond in the center of you, the diamond of the awakened heart. Your heart is pure and brilliant. Your heart is your true self. This true self is untainted by past experiences. It waits for you to connect to and reveal the diamond-like clarity and brilliance of your beautiful, awakened heart. When you uncover the diamond, you let its brilliant light shine powerfully. One common purpose that is shared by all is the desire to be happy and the inherent want/need to overcome suffering. No one truly wants to live in pain or in a state of disconnection. To achieve happiness is to overcome suffering and return to our natural state of being. The question then becomes: How do we achieve this?

The Four Noble Truths

1.Suffering exists. In order to change anything you first have to acknowledge the problem.

In Buddhism, suffering is discomfort, dissatisfaction or unhappiness. It is part of being human to feel discomfort. During our lifetime, each of us will have to experience physical discomforts such as pain, sickness, injury, tiredness, old age and eventually death. Each of us will experience psychological discomfort through emotions like sadness, fear, frustration, disappointment, and depression. These experiences are viewed as the "such-ness" of human existence. The first noble truth is the acknowledgement of discomfort and dissatisfaction as a truth of the human existence.

2. Suffering comes from within ourselves; it is created by the mind and perceptions.

The origin of suffering is attachment to transient or external things as a means to happiness. Transient things do not only include the physical objects that surround us, but also ideas and -in a greater sense- all objects of our perception. The reasons for suffering are desire, passion, the want of more and more, the pursuit of wealth and prestige, the striving for fame and popularity, or in short: *craving* and *clinging.* Because the objects of our attachment are transient, their loss is inevitable. Thus, suffering will follow. Seeking happiness, security and pleasure from the external changing world is the cause of suffering and dis-satisfaction.

With faith all things are possible. ᏩᏫ

3. Suffering has an end. Change yourself, change your
mind and end suffering.

The end of suffering comes from *learning to restrain and develop the mind*. This means that suffering can be overcome simply by removing the cause of suffering, by learning to NOT identify solely with the "things" of this life. This Noble Truth tells us that peace, happiness and freedom from suffering is possible. You already have the very things you are seeking. Happiness, comfort, peace, tranquility and security lie within the hearts of us all; these qualities are inherent to our true nature. In your heart, you are and you have all of these things.

4. There is a path that ends the cycles suffering.
Happiness is the path.

The way to end of suffering is the middle way, the place between the two extremes of excessive over-indulgence and excessive disregard. By following the Noble middle path, suffering ends and that leads to peace, happiness, wisdom and enlightenment. By choosing to live from the heart, our true nature, is to choose the path of happiness. The path of happiness is a knowing that I cannot seek happiness in the world of impermanence; happiness comes from within. Achieve happiness by cultivating the positive qualities within yourself. Have faith in the fundamental goodness at the core of your being. Nothing in the world can touch this well of happiness, peace and faith. When you understand this, you will be free.

The Four Noble Truths give us faith that there is a way out of suffering. In order for a sick person to get well, the first step is to acknowledge they are ill. This will naturally lead the individual to discover what led to this condition and what is making it worse. When this has been discovered, the person wishes to be free of the illness and will seek remedies. Therefore first and foremost, it is essential to acknowledge the present state of suffering, or struggle, in order to change it. Then you have to choose to live in new ways, the ways that heal. The Noble middle path is a

FAITH IN BUDDHISM

way of living that connects each individual to the fundamental goodness contained within the diamond heart. It
is the choice to live a life of freedom and happiness.

In 2006, I made a conscious decision to find a teacher and
step more formally onto the path of Buddhism. My teacher of
reiki was also a Buddhist practitioner. I was intrigued by her
wisdom, moved by her compassion and touched by her ability to
wake things up in me. She stirred the little Buddha inside me as
she taught me reiki. I did some research in order to find a Buddhist teacher of my own. I found a teacher that was located close
to me, just an hour away that I felt drawn to. Coincidentally,
this Buddhist teacher was the teacher of the woman I was working with. Synchronicity in action.

I reached out to him and we set up a time to meet. I was ner-
vous, yet excited on so many levels. I had faith that I was on the
right path and was being guided to the right teacher. When I met
Lama, there was no pretense; I showed up with two kids in tow
~ a 4-year-old and a 1-year-old. I showed up as a mom, I showed
up as I was.

Lama is a revered teacher from Nepal. He is a man of few
words, but the words he speaks have immense power. I was an in-
quisitive and challenging student. I wanted everything from him.
What he helped me to I realize is that I had everything inside of
me. I did not know this right away, but through his guidance and
through study I came to realize I had everything I needed inside
of me. This is the beauty of Buddhism, that there is no need for
self-improvement when you know your true self; you know there is
no need to suffer, because there is a way out of suffering.

In one of our first meetings I felt the need to share my story
with my teacher. I recounted my past, the highs and lows. I
shared with him the difficulties I had experienced and the pain I
still carried within me. He listened quietly, with a gentleness flowing from his eyes. I knew there was no judgment and only love. I
finished my story and he was silent. I thought he would expound
some great teaching upon me, or that he would at least confirm
that I had suffered and struggled.

I was surprised by his response. He simply sat across me with
complete compassion and acceptance and said, "And now?" He

was pointing out that I was still suffering and struggling because I was bringing the past into the now. Yes, the pain had been experienced, but the suffering was optional. I was only suffering because I was identifying with the past and with pain. It was time for me to wake up and get in touch with the warmth and brilliance that was right before my eyes. In the blink of an eye, I could wake up to the fundamental goodness, compassion and wisdom that is me. I could be free; liberation was within my reach.

The word *Buddha* means "the awakened one." In the story of the Buddha, it is told that after much dedication and discovery, the Buddha reached enlightenment and attained the understandings contained within the Four Noble Truths. The Buddha then set out into the world to share these teachings with others, to guide others out of suffering. The Buddha had just *woken up*, had just become a Buddha, when he encountered a man on the road who was struck by his extraordinary level of peace and presence.

He asked the Buddha, "What are you, my friend? Are you a celestial being or God?"
The Buddha replied, "No."
He asked the Buddha, "Are you some kind of magician or wizard?"
The Buddha replied, "No."
He asked the Buddha, "Are you a man?"
The Buddha replied, "No."
"Well then, my friend, what are you?"
The Buddha replied, "I am awake."

The understandings and teachings offered on the path of Buddhism are meant to wake you up to the virtues of the heart and the power of faith, the power of compassion, the power of love and to wake you up to the power of insight. The Buddha taught that, in order to be free, you must first understand why you suffer and be taught the practical means to move out of suffering. The path of Buddhism develops faith in the power of compassion, loving kindness and wisdom as means to leave behind suffering. Have faith in the diamond of the heart and the ability of the heart to open and shine. Have faith in

FAITH IN BUDDHISM

the ability of the heart to transform and heal the world. Have faith that there is a little Buddha inside of you, one who is *awake*.

Further teachings on faith are offered in the Buddhist text,

Avatamsaka Sutra:
Faith is the basis of the Path, the mother of virtues,
Nourishing and growing all good ways,
Cutting away the net of doubt, freeing from the torrent of passion,
Revealing the unsurpassed road of ultimate peace.

When faith is undefiled, the mind is pure;
Obliterating pride, it is the root of reverence,
And the foremost wealth in the treasury of religion ...

Faith is generous ...
Faith can joyfully enter the Buddha's teaching;
Faith can increase knowledge and virtue;
Faith can ensure arrival at enlightenment ...
Faith can go beyond the pathways of demons,
And reveal the unsurpassed road of liberation.

Faith is the unspoiled seed of virtue,
Faith can grow the seed of enlightenment.
Faith can increase supreme knowledge,
Faith can reveal all Buddhas ...
Faith is most powerful, very difficult to have;
It's like in all worlds having the wondrous wish-fulfilling pearl.
Bodhisattva Samantabhadra

Faith is explained as the mother of virtues. Virtues are the ground on which we stand; they govern our actions and guide our conduct. Faith is the ground under your feet. Each time you stand on this ground you are nourished and you grow in all good ways. Every experience is a part of the ground you stand on. Have faith; this ground is lifting you up to new heights and is your path to liberation. These past experiences are not over you, they are under you, lifting you up, giving you something to stand on. They are a part of the path moving you toward the highest heights, the heights of love, happiness and peace. They are the experiences on the road to enlightenment and liberation.

Faith can ensure your arrival at enlightenment. Living in enlightenment is living a life full of light. It is a life of wisdom, peace and happiness. Living in enlightenment is living awake. Living in enlightenment is being connected to your diamond heart, your awakened heart. Faith must be the basis of the path. Have faith that there is a place in your heart that is *awake*. Have faith that there is a place within you untainted by your past experiences and the pain of living in the world. Develop a wisdom that understands that all have experienced pain; it is part of the human experience. Develop a wisdom that knows freedom from suffering is possible. Understand that you can be free from your past, free from the darkness and disconnection. Be courageous enough to stand on the path open-hearted and awake, and fully connected to the power of faith. In faith, supreme knowledge increases.

Develop faith through experience and commitment. Faith is one of the most difficult virtues to develop, for it is a result of trusting. It asks you to trust in a practice before you see the results. Trust in the power of compassion to alleviate anger before you are free from anger. Trust in the power of loving kindness to transform a relationship before the relationship is transformed. Trust in the fact that a diamond is planted at the core of your heart before you have unearthed it.

Having faith in a heart that is filled with compassion and loving kindness inspires you to go in search of such a heart and to uncover the treasure of the diamond heart.

FAITH IN BUDDHISM

Apply the Lesson
GETTING IN TOUCH
WITH LOVING KINDNESS

Meditation:

Metta meditation is a practice for healing the heart. It is the practice of loving kindness. It is a beautiful and simple practice of wishing well for yourself and all others. Below is a modified version of the classic practice.

Find yourself in a comfortable environment, somewhere with minimum distractions so that you can be undisturbed for a period of time. Sit comfortably either on the floor or in a chair. If you are seated on the floor, have blankets or pillows under your bottom for support. If you are seated in a chair, either gather the legs under you or have the feet firmly planted upon the ground.

Sit with the spine straight and your heart lifted to the heavens. Let your eyes softly close and take a few moments to become quiet and attentive to the breath.

Continue in this manner for 5 to 10 minutes.

Take a deep breath in and bring your hands to touch in front of the heart.

Begin to repeat these statements, offering loving kindness to yourself:

- "May I be happy."

- "May I be healthy."

- "May I live with ease of heart."

- "May I have faith in all of life."

Continue in this way for 5 minutes.

With faith all things are possible.

Bring to mind someone you love or are concerned about, offering loving kindness to them:

- ✸ "May you be happy."
- ✸ "May you be healthy."
- ✸ "May you live with ease of heart."
- ✸ "May you have faith in all of life."

Continue in this way for 5 minutes.

Extend this loving kindness out to all beings:

- ✸ "May all beings be happy."
- ✸ "May all beings be healthy."
- ✸ "May all beings live with ease of heart."
- ✸ "May all beings have faith in all of life."

Continue in this way for 5 minutes.

When you are ready, take a deep breath and gently allow your eyes to open. Take out your journal and write down your responses:

- ✸ What is happiness to me?
- ✸ What does it mean to be healthy?
- ✸ How would it feel to live my life with ease of heart?
- ✸ What does it mean to live with faith in all my life?

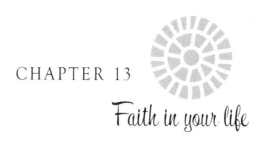

CHAPTER 13

Faith in your life

*"When you realize how perfect everything is, you will tilt
your head back and laugh at the sky." Buddha*

Living in alignment with faith is living in alignment with purpose. It is living from the heart. It is inspiring others, and it is using all the gifts, talents and abilities that were placed in you upon conception to fulfill your divine purpose. Uncommon faith transforms difficulty into purpose and turmoil into triumph. Living in alignment with faith is the ability to be the soul of the place where you stand, courageous enough to stand tall and shine your light brightly. When you live on purpose, you can be nothing other than the soul of the place you stand. When you live on purpose, you bring a level of excellence to everything you do and everyone you meet. You are the example of the earth walk of faith. You are the example of how to have unshakeable trust in the whole of life and the perfection of the universe. Living on purpose is to use your light and wisdom to guide others toward their power and purpose.

Awakening for one reveals the power and potential for awakening in all. Living in alignment with divine purpose is not about your job, the work you do in the world, but about what you bring to that work. Living in alignment with faith means being willing to accept and act upon the guidance from within that asks you to do things that may not make sense or seem logical from where you are. Uncommon faith trusts in what is meant for you, the bigger vision; the vision of purpose. A person of uncommon faith is bold enough to do the work that brings this vision to life. Faith is the bedrock of strength that you must stand upon to live in alignment with your divine purpose.

By redefining and understanding your life from a level of uncommon faith, you will know that each experience has a divine purpose and that you have a divine purpose. Everyone is born with a purpose; therefore, understand that all your experiences are taking you one step closer to living consciously in alignment with your purpose. Learn to live in the light of love. Share with others what you have learned. Share with others the gifts of experiences. See each experience ~ the great ones and the not so great ones ~ as a gift to you.

Tami came to my office dressed to the nines; from the outside it looked like she had it all together. Her clothes were sharp, the high heels perfectly matched, hair in place and a smile on her face. Yet, right behind that, when you looked just a little deeper, there was an uneasiness to her, as if her foundation was quaking. Tami, a divorced mother of 2, was struggling in her life in many areas. She was working night and day to keep her independent business going in order to provide for her children. She was facing some real challenges in navigating divorce and the emotional destruction the divorce had left behind. She had somehow made her way to me in order to get some guidance and care. She was experiencing increased levels of anxiety and unhappiness.

The first step was awareness. As Tami spoke about the troubles that had brought her to me ~ the troubles with her "was-band" the ex, the troubles with sleep, the troubles with focus, the troubles in her life ~ I patiently watched all of these troubles manifest physically. She shook, tapped her foot, clicked her pen; she was unable to be still. She had a strong faith, but she had lost touch with its power. Fear had taken over.

In our work, I asked Tami to pay attention to the places she was investing her energy. Where our minds go, our energy flows. She was allowing her energy to flow to her troubles without being aware of the impact it was having on her. As she focused her energy, she became empowered to calm the anxiety and calm herself. Faith is ever present, right in the middle of the chaos. Faith sits at the center of the hurricane, the quiet calm at the middle of your being. As Tami learned to calm and claim her power back, her faith was renewed and restored. Faith was restored at the center of her life, and in that she has found her way out of the storm and is living the life that is meant for her: the life of success, love and, most of all, peace and happiness.

Faith-filled testimonial

"I was a walking shell. After years of emotional abuse, my self-esteem was a faint memory. This coming from a woman who once earned six figures and was a top sales executive and still didn't think she was good enough. The people who were supposed to love me made me feel this way, with my permission. I felt I was in a free fall with responsibilities and demands pulling at me in ways I couldn't control. The anxiety and fear overcame me.

I had faith in God; I knew that if I would allow myself I could be guided in greater ways. I needed to get in touch with my heart and soul again. My pastor once told me I could run toward God in trying times and I could allow him to work great things in me, or I could run from him and try to figure it out on my own.

I chose faith. That meant I had to trust again, I had to let go and be guided. I had to endure the agony of self-growth. I had to accept my shortcomings and remember my strengths. I had to own this journey. I have to admit, the dark paths of self-discovery were very scary and I felt I was on a faith treadmill with no end in sight.

Felicia and I started peeling back the emotional layers. Over the next few months, I was reminded that I matter. I realized this journey was a life lesson: I learned to respond, no longer react. I learned to be grateful for the little things. Then with time, gratefulness became a part of my inner dialog. I learned that I control my energy and what is attracted to me. I learned to say 'No, thank you' to insults, instigations, negativity, fear. I learned to say 'Yes, please' to small gestures, compliments, even a roast beef sample at Publix (I don't even like roast beef).

One day, in divine timing, when I was ready, negativity subsided, the fog lifted, the fear dissipated. In its place, abundance, love, light, joy, and now, peace prevailed. I now trust again wholeheartedly, thanks to my journey of Uncommon Faith."

Tami S.

When you realize how perfectly designed the universe is, how each piece of your life has come together to form the beautiful design of your life, you can tilt your head back and laugh. You can open your heart and heal. Have faith in the design of the universe. Have faith in the order of the universe. Have faith in yourself, and let that faith evolve to ever-deepening and expansive power. Uncommon faith is a degree of faith you know, without a doubt, that you are important. You know, without doubt, that all things that you have experienced are important for your evolution and growth. Uncommon faith is unbreakable; this degree of faith allows the heavens to bring you the blessings of faith. Uncommon faith activates the energy that brings you blessings. Where you are, good or bad, is not the end of the road. There are so many great things you are meant to do and be. Walk forward in faith; let faith be your guide.

Uncommon faith is unshakable faith. Once an individual understands faith from the unshakable level, faith takes on a new meaning. Faith becomes very personal, and it is the underlying wisdom that guides you forth on your path, the foundation of all decision making. Develop a personal relationship with faith ~ not as a concept, but by choosing faith in moments of doubt or fear. In that, you experience life in the energy of faith. Choosing faith will transform long-held, outdated beliefs. When you change from within, your life will transform in amazing ways. With uncommon faith, you can let go of beliefs that have held you back, overcome fears and live a life on purpose.

Every time you choose to act in uncommon faith and say yes, what you experience is magical. Love and support enter your life when your heart is open. The past can be the past. I describe healing as being in the present moment, free of the past and unattached to the future. It is being free of fear and worry. It is being faith-filled, faith-guided and faithfully dedicated to the practices that bring inspiration and liberation.

> *"The Buddha said, 'Faith is the beginning of all good things.' No matter what we encounter in life, it is faith that enables us to try again, to trust again, and to love again. Even in times of immense suffering, it is faith that enables us to relate to the present moment in such a way that we can go on, we can move forward, instead of becoming lost in resignation or despair."* Sharon Salzberg

In times of struggle and pain, faith enables you to relate to the present moment openly and honestly so you can move forward, instead of becoming lost in despair. Faith links our present-day experiences, whether wonderful or terrible, to the underlying pulse of life itself. Uncommon faith is unbreakable and indestructible; it is the foundation you stand upon. Have faith in your divine purpose, the purpose behind each experience you have encountered, and all the rest to come. Having faith in a universe that is for you will allow you to transform the way you see each person, situation and experience. You will see them through the eyes of the soul, which is wise and loving and guides you at all times. Faith is ignited the moment you decide to try again, to make a conscious step into the unknown.

Faith is an antidote to fear. Fear is living in a state of disconnection. Fear pushes away and has aversion to the present moment. Fear tells us that things are insurmountable, and why even try? Uncommon faith knows you are always supported, and you can move forward, especially when you don't know how you will. Uncommon faith is the quality that makes truth your own and not some abstract idea you have read about. In this process you learn to trust in yourself, learn to trust in your courage and learn to trust in your strength. Have faith that you are strong enough to face life open-hearted. In faith, let each moment arise just as it is. This teaches you that you are far more powerful than you realize; this is the knowing of faith. In the energy of doubt and fear, we pull back and don't even try. Being afraid to fail keeps you from trusting your vision, guidance and heart.

Faith is trust. With faith, trust in the power you contain. Trust that you have a divine purpose. Trust in your power to bring your dreams to life. Uncommon faith is the power to dream big and trust that all you need will be provided. Your dedication, your faith, has the power to move mountains and overcome any obstacle. With a mustard seed of faith, nothing can hold you back.

Faith is confidence. When you face a daunting task, have confidence, have faith that you will succeed. Confidence is required to live your purpose, confidence so strong that no setback shakes you from your path or your purpose. As you begin to live life in new way, a lot of restlessness, resistance and pain may come forward. Change can be difficult, and it tests you in innumerable ways. Faith and confidence are essential to your success. Uncommon faith gives you the confidence to keep moving forward and navigate through the changes that are necessary to put you in alignment with your purpose.

Faith is patience. Patience means being willing to be present in a situation and allowing it to unfold without manipulating it. Patience is letting things take their natural course. Uncommon faith trusts in the perfection of the moment. Have faith enough to be patient with the process of change. Stay committed, yet unattached, to the outcome. The plan of the divine tends to far exceed our plan. With patience, there is no resistance to what life is offering you. With faith, divine timing ~ allowing things to happen when the time is right ~ is honored and understood. Divine timing is to allow things to happen when the time is right. It is patience in the waiting, faith in the moment. With patience, you are willing to stay committed to the changes necessary for you to live on purpose. There is no need to rush, because every experience is a precious moment and honored as important. The patience of faith knows everything is as it should be. This kind of patience requires faith. It requires faith in the bigger picture of life, the visionary quality of faith.

Faith is courage. Courageous enough to step away from the normal dictates of society and the way it defines happiness, success and prosperity. Living on purpose breaks the bonds of limitation, and it takes courage to step away from what others want for you. Courageous faith boldly steps forward and takes action. To live in alignment with purpose takes a courageous aspect of faith that is by no means insignificant. With faith, your courage is magnified and you will take risks and dare to dream big. Uncommon faith is the freedom to dream big.

Ultimately, we must have faith in ourselves and the wisdom and divinity within us. Faith allows us to trust our intuitive awareness, and it strengthens our connection to each other and ourselves. Uncommon faith is the earth walk of faith: moving forward on the path with courage, trust, patience, compassion and truth. Have faith in your heart, your vision and dreams. Look squarely at life with the eyes of faith, for you are exactly where you need to be.

With just a mustard seed of faith, you can move mountains, overcome any difficulty, transform any adversity and live an extraordinary life. You can live a life of purpose, a life of wonder and a life of amazement. You will learn to step to the edge of all you know and trust. Trust that one of two things will happen: there will be something solid to stand on, or you will be taught to fly. When you are faced with a challenge or blessed with a gift, stay in faith. When you are in the highs or lows of life, stay in faith.

The people you admire and the vision you see them living out is a result of the daily earth walk of faith. It is each day moving past doubts, fears and limitations. It is

FAITH IN YOUR LIFE

each day aligning to and acting on faith. It takes faith to bring dreams to life. It takes the level of uncommon faith that this book is guiding you to develop. A dream stays in the realm of imagination without purposeful action. Uncommon faith, faith in action, is what turns imagination into reality. As I have allowed myself to heal from the past, I have learned the power of faith in action. I have seen my life expand in ways I could never have imagined. The divine plan of the heavens has far exceeded my plans. I have seen this mustard seed of faith take over the lands of my heart. The mustard seed of faith has moved mountains in my life. It is the superpower that transforms any obstacle into an opportunity. It is the superpower that you have access to in each moment you choose faith over fear.

Growing up in a home void of spirituality and with the belief that life just happens created a space for me to explore. I see this as a gift. I carried no dogma about any right path. I was eager to learn and needed to explore in order to heal. It allowed me to go in search of meaning and in search of understanding. I needed to make sense of my difficulties and the trauma of the past. Without understanding, I was left living in pain. This pain ended up being a great gift; it propelled me to discovery. It was the catalyst of my awakening. It was the catalyst for my deep healing and growth. I set out in search of relief, and I found the treasure of faith. I know with certainty that my faith has always been with me and within me. Having faith has made me the woman I am today.

Each path I have explored ultimately led me back to the same place time and time again, the sacred space of my heart, the core of my being. Each path has led me back to the diamond of the heart, the treasure house of divine powers on this planet. You are the divine, the spirit here on this planet, developing your earth walk of faith. You are a divine spiritual being having a human experience. This experience is meant to develop your faith to the level of uncommon faith, where all things of the heavens are possible in your

With faith all things are possible. ⟲

life. The doors of faith are opened within you, through discovery of "*Who am I?*" and "*What I am here for?*"

Yoga opened the doors of faith through the powers of connection and presence. Yoga taught me about having faith in my body, my mind, my heart and soul. I came to the practice feeling lost and broken. The practice teaches that you are never lost when you learn to come home to yourself, to the divine light in your heart. Yoga took me from feeling broken to the experience of union. The yoga practice united my body, mind and soul. The union of yoga is the wholeness we seek at the core of our being.

Reiki taught me about healing. First and foremost, it taught me how to heal myself. Reiki put the power of healing in my hands. Reiki taught me that I could end the cycle of pain by changing my vibration one thought at a time and one choice at a time. When I changed my vibration, my life began to change dramatically. Reiki takes faith. Reiki energy is intangible, yet has a power that cannot be denied. Reiki connected me to my divine purpose of helping to heal others. This is done by healing. The compassion and understanding I have experienced though the vibration of reiki changed me in powerful ways. This superpower of compassion is what I tap into and access through reiki as I assist others in healing.

Reiki opened my heart to the promise of healing. Reiki is a connection to the source of light, healing and faith. Reiki offers faith that there is a place within you that is already whole. By surrendering and healing the past, you encounter wholeness. Wholeness is health, well-being and peace. Reiki teaches you to have faith that healing is possible, and faith in your ability to allow healing to happen.

Buddhism taught me to have faith in my heart and the compassion and kindness carried within it. The path of Buddhism gave me an understanding about the nature of life itself. Buddhism is a path of heart and a path of awakening. Buddhism is a path built on faith and awakening the heart, which is the source of faith. When I came to Buddhism, I was trying to discover the bigger thing I

FAITH IN YOUR LIFE

am meant to have faith in. Buddhism taught me, first and foremost, about myself and the beauty I contain. This beautiful, compassionate and kind being is easy to express on the other side of suffering. Buddhism showed me a way out of suffering. Buddhism allowed me to understand the power of commitment, compassion and loving-kindness.

Buddhism led me to the doors of my heart and opened them wide. Subsequently, these doors have opened me to an ever-deepening relationship to God. The path of Buddhism brought me back to God and the Angels. I have chosen, in faith, to explore, in an unlimited and wonderful way, the magical connection to the source of all. When you choose faith, you choose to live a path of purpose. Faith is worth investing in. Choose faith each day. See the power of faith unfold in your life.

"Faith is the beauty of your heart.

Faith is the light in the dark.

Faith is the answer to your prayers.

Faith is the antidote to fear.

Faith is trust.

Faith is confidence.

Faith is patience.

Faith is courage.

Faith is power.

Faith is love.

Faith is in you."

-Felicia McQuaid

⌒⌒ Apply the Lesson

GETTING IN TOUCH WITH WHAT IS FAITH

Meditation:

Find yourself in a comfortable environment, somewhere with minimum distractions so that you can be undisturbed for a period of time. Sit comfortably either on the floor or in a chair. If you are seated on the floor, have blankets or pillows under your bottom for support. If you are seated in a chair, either gather the legs under you or have the feet firmly planted upon the ground.

Sit with the spine straight, attentive to your posture. Let your eyes softly close and take a few moments to become quiet and attentive to the breath. With each breath, relax more deeply and open more fully.

Continue in this manner for 5 to 10 minutes.

Contemplate "What is faith?"

Pay attention to the thoughts, words, phrases, images, sensations and emotions that arise as you contemplate this question. Simply breathe, observe and listen. There are no wrong answers; this is not about getting the answer right, just the simple contemplation of faith.

Continue in this manner for 5 to 10 minutes.

Take a deep breath in and a deep breath out.

Declare these statements quietly inside.

Repeat each phrase three times:

☀ "Faith is the beginning of all good things."

☀ "Faith is bold."

☀ "Faith is courageous."

☀ "Faith is trusting."

☀ "Faith is confident."

- "Faith is patient."
- "Faith is powerful."
- "Faith is beauty."
- "Faith is light."
- "Faith is the answer to my prayers."

When you are ready, take a deep breath and gently allow your eyes to open. Take out your journal and write down your responses:

- What does faith mean to me?
- What do I have faith in about myself?
- Has this answer changed from the first response in Chapter 1?
- In what ways?

With faith all things are possible.

CHAPTER 14

Faith in divine purpose

*"Lift your gaze to the light, to the possibility of freedom,
and to the possibility that the difficulty of the past has a
great purpose and meaning." Felicia McQuaid*

This book has been lifetimes in the making. Uncommon faith is the result of maturity, dedication and practice. It is the daily choice to walk the earth walk of faith. Faith is easy in the "easy times," when everything is going the way we think it should be. Faith is developed when we are challenged the most. This book is an offering of faith. It is the challenge to share my story and the wisdom of the paths I have explored. Uncommon faith has developed in the midst of adversity, uncertainty, pain and doubt. Uncommon faith is the light in the dark that guides you in all ways.

This book is my greatest act of uncommon faith thus far. I have no guarantee of the impact and effect this book will have in the world. What I do know is that it will have an impact, and I have been guided to share my story and share my wisdom in a bold and purpose-filled way. I have practiced uncommon faith with each word. I have practiced faith in the power of the words I write. These are the words I am guided to write, the stories I have been guided to reveal and the power of the wisdom I have obtained along the way. It is to have faith in myself, to step up and out to something I have not attempted before, such as writing a book. I had faith that I would eventually write a book. This became uncommon faith the moment I began. This uncommon faith has deepened with each chapter.

My personal story has been hidden within me for so long, just as yours may be. I have faith in its purpose, and I have faith that my story has the power to inspire others to reveal and heal their story; the power to transform the past right here, right now. I have an inner knowing, an unshakable, unbreakable level of understanding of the importance of healing and stepping forward in a new way. It is a way of purpose, a way of peace and a way of wisdom. I have a certainty of knowing around the power of faith. It is from maturity and experiencing the power of the heavens working in my life in amazing ways. I have a certainty of knowing that if healing is available to one person; it is equally available to everyone.

> *"The kingdom of Heaven is like a*
> *mustard seed planted in a field.*
> *It is the smallest of all the seeds, but it*
> *grows into the largest of garden plants,*
> *It grows into a tree and birds come and*
> *make nests in its branches.*
> *If you have faith even as small as a*
> *mustard seed, you can say to the mountain,*
> *'Move from here to there' and it would move.*
> *Nothing would be impossible." Matthew 17:20*

Just a mustard seed of faith and you can move mountains, overcome any difficulty, transform any adversity and live an extraordinary life. You can live a life of purpose, wonder and amazement. You will learn to step to the edge of all you know and trust and one of two things will happen: There will be something solid for us to stand on, or we will be taught to fly.

I have a certainty of knowing, a faith-filled knowing, that if I can heal and live on divine purpose, so can anyone who chooses faith and acts on it. Anyone can experience this level of uncommon faith. Dedicate your whole heart to yourself, to your life and to finding and living in alignment with your purpose.

With faith all things are possible. ⊙⟋

Learn to make a difference where you stand, in your home, in your community and any place you find yourself. To choose is to begin. Have uncommon faith and step out, step up and know that all will be shown to you and all will be provided for you. This is not an overnight process; it will take time and dedication. It will take effort, but the rewards are great. Invest in faith and be courageous and dedicated enough to allow this energy to unfold in your life in amazing and monumental ways.

Whatever your challenge, know there is a power stronger than that challenge: the power of your faith. When you are grounded in faith, you have a knowing that this has purpose. You will ask, *"What are you here to teach me?"* You will learn and you will grow. The ground of faith is the bedrock of your strength. Standing in faith is a knowing that you are not doing this alone. When Joshua stood on the battleground and was bold enough to ask for the sun to stop in the sky, he did not stop fighting. He kept doing his work and had faith that he was supported, and he was! Uncommon faith activates supernatural powers. Think of it like this:

Natural Power (individual) + FAITH = Supernatural Powers (individual and universe working together)

Joshua and God working together to defeat the enemy!

Step boldly into new territory and have faith that you are supported. Allow for freedom and expansion by opening up to the possibility of it. It is extraordinary living in the midst of daily, ordinary life. Sound big? It is! That is what faith is about: daring to dream, being bold enough to ask and being brave enough to act. It is big!

Just a mustard seed of faith and you will see the power of faith working in your life. Share your success with others. Have faith in others. Speak in words of faith. Encourage the efforts you are making, and stay dedicated. The process of transformation does not happen

FAITH IN DIVINE PURPOSE

overnight. It takes time. When in times of doubt, return to these words; remind yourself of where you have been and how far you have come already. That is uncommon faith! Share your stories and experiences with others. I have faith that my story will uplift and inspire at least one person. Maybe that one person is you. If so, thank you for letting me live out my divine purpose! I have *faith* in you, my friend.

> *Faith is the all-encompassing superpower*
> *of the universe. Trust in it, just a tiny bit,*
> *and you will see. Step forward, dare to*
> *walk the earth walk of faith.*

⟡ *Apply the Lesson*
GETTING IN TOUCH
WITH UNCOMMON FAITH

Meditation:

Find yourself in a comfortable environment, somewhere with minimum distractions so that you can be undisturbed for a period of time. Sit comfortably either on the floor or in a chair. If you are seated on the floor, have blankets or pillows under your bottom for support. If you are seated in a chair, either gather the legs under you or have the feet firmly planted upon the ground.

Sit with the spine straight, attentive to your posture. Let your eyes softly close and take a few moments to become quiet and attentive to the breath. Let your hands rest on your lap with the tip of the thumb and index finger touching on each hand. As you breathe, simply connect to the breath flowing in and the breath flowing out. Thoughts will come and thoughts will come but you remain undisturbed by simply observing the breath. Witness and observe the breath. Continue in this way for 5 to 10 minutes.

Contemplate your bold declaration of faith, your bold vision of your future. Bring to mind the dream that you want to see in your reality. See it as if it were already in reality, as if it were already in your life.

* How would that feel?

* What would it look like? Give your vision, your dreams a real life image, what it would look like in your world.

* What would it be as a career? What changes would it create for your family? How would you look? What would your daily life be like?

Simply breathe, contemplate and observe.
Continue in this way for 5 to 10 minutes.

FAITH IN DIVINE PURPOSE

Take a deep breath in and declare these intentions for your day. "Today I choose to act in the power of uncommon faith by ..."

- "Choosing to live boldly."

- "Choosing to dream big."

- "Choosing to succeed."

- "Choosing to prosper."

- "Choosing to speak kindly."

- "Choosing to live wisely."

- "Choosing to live compassionately."

- "And above all, "Choosing faith over fear!"

- "With faith all things are possible."

When you are ready, take a deep breath and gently allow your eyes to open. Take out your journal and write down your responses:

- In alignment with the power of faith, today I choose to act in the power of faith by

  _____

- Pick one of the statements from your meditation and put it into practice today!

- Make a commitment to live in the power of uncommon faith by action!

Frequently Asked Questions ❦

Q: Will doubt still arise? What then?

A: Doubt is a product of fear. It is natural and very human to feel scared, especially when making a bold move in your life. I have learned over the years, when doubts have arisen, to use this energy to develop my faith. What am I actually doubting? Do I doubt my abilities? Do I doubt I will receive the support I need? Doubt can be used to clear out any blind spots. It is not wrong to feel fear or have doubts. Acting on fear and doubts is natural, but will lead you off track. Examine the doubt, investigate and weed out the belief that is limiting you, and then choose faith over fear.

Q: What is the true meaning of walking in faith?

A: The earth walk of faith is being willing to stand in your life exactly where you are, open-hearted and faith-filled. This means in the easy times, when faith is easy, and in the difficult times. This is when standing in faith is most needed and the most difficult to do. The earth walk of faith trusts and knows that each experience, each person, each moment and each day is purposeful and purpose-filled. The earth walk of faith is walking boldly toward your dreams and being amazed at the beauty of the process of discovery.

Q: What can I do daily to renew my faith?

A: Simple. Make time for quiet, sacred time each day. Take time each day to listen, to ask for the guidance you need, and then receive it. Prayer is talking to the divine; meditation is listening. Begin each day with an intention for your day.

"Today I will walk in faith. I am open to the beauty of this day."

Your quiet time may not be sitting in lotus position on a meditation cushion; maybe it is a morning walk in nature, a run or a swim. Most importantly, create a space that cares for you and allows you to connect to you.

Q: What path of healing is best for me?

A: Each person is unique; I can only offer what I have experienced as effective in my healing path. I would say explore, explore, explore. When you feel drawn to explore something, check it out. I had no idea what yoga was truly about, but I felt drawn to it. Everywhere I went I saw the word; fliers jumped off boards at me, and people asked me, "Have you ever tried yoga?"

As a teacher of healing practices, I hear so many stories from people who end up in my clinic because they had a feeling, or someone had mentioned my name to them for the third time. I often hear them say, "I have no idea what this reiki stuff is, but I feel like it can help me." Step out of your comfort zone and try something new; you may be amazed by what happens.

Alternative care should never replace conventional medical care, but may be supplemental to conventional treatment provided by a qualified physician. When seeking an alternative care therapist, do your research and make sure they are licensed by the state you live in and are highly qualified in their field of study.

Q: I've tried before, so why try again?

A: Every time we attempt something new, it is from a new place. You cannot step into the same river twice. Understand that nothing is truly ever the same; limited perception makes it look that way. The past is only in the present moment when it is brought there. So first, give yourself more credit!

You have learned more than you realize. The first time you go to the gym, you are sore, you are not able to lift the biggest weight in the gym, but you are stronger each time you work out. The first time you run, you start with a block, and you are tired. But a month later, because of dedication, you are running a mile and still breathing. Don't give up, because ultimately, giving up is giving up on yourself. You are a powerful, divine individual. Without faith, what do we have? Without faith in yourself, life loses its beauty and luster, and so do you.

With faith all things are possible. ⌒⌒

Q: Is faith tangible?

A: The very nature of faith is to open up to something that is beyond physical, tangible reality. Those driven by limited views and limited beliefs only believe it when they see it. Faith asks us to stand at the edge of all we know and be willing to take a step forward, without a guarantee of outcome. Faith is so trusting and powerful that it moves you past all limitations. It allows you to exceed the limits of your beliefs and stand in alignment with the soul force inside you. The soul is real. Is it tangible? The tangibility, for me, comes after you act in the energy of faith. The tangibility is seen when your dreams come to life.

Q: Without faith, what do we have?

A: Without faith in yourself, life loses it beauty and luster, and so do you. Without faith, my life felt aimless, and I felt lost. I saw myself floating from experience to experience, feeling beaten and battered. Faith empowers individuals. It is a power that is hard to express in words, but it feels like suddenly standing up within your life in a conscious way.

Without connection to my faith, I would settle for less than I deserve and choose a small life. Without my faith, my life would lack color. I'd be content to watch black and white TV, not truly knowing how beautiful and colorful life can be. Faith adds color to your life. It brings feelings of peace and inspiration. Faith is the voice of encouragement from within.

In actuality, we are never without faith; it is always there.

Q: Why choose faith above all else?

A: Faith is the foundation of all the other virtues. Faith allows hope to thrive. Faith allows love to flow. Faith allows for connection. Faith allows for courage. You must first develop faith in yourself, not the limited you, but the *true* you, the one that is braver than you know and stronger than you think. When you have faith in this part of yourself, the beauty and light within you, it develops faith in something bigger. With faith, you understand that you are an integral and important part of life itself. Faith asks you to trust in things you cannot see. First trust in the soul within you that you cannot see. When you can do that, you can trust in the other forces of the universe that you cannot see.

Q: I still don't know my purpose. Can you define purpose further for me? How do I live my life on purpose daily?

A: Every moment of every day is the practice of living on purpose. One common purpose that each individual shares is to be happy ~ a level of happiness that is sustainable and fulfilling, that exists even when things are not under our control. Examine your daily life and ask, "Is this situation, job or person contributing to my happiness?" Happiness is a sense of connection and peace. When you feel happy or you contribute to the happiness of another, it spreads. The ultimate divine purpose of your life is not separate from what makes you happy; it is directly connected to it. When you find your purpose, it is pleasing to the soul. It makes you smile from within.

Go out today and spread joy, bring happiness to everything you do and uplift everyone you meet. Divine purpose is not about the job you have and the roles you play throughout your day and life ~ the roles of friend, sister, brother, boss, parent; the list is endless. Rather, it is about the energy brought to and through those things. Start where you are and see where that leads you.

With faith all things are possible. ⟳

About Joanna Cotten

Country music singer Joanna Cotten is the muse behind McQuaid's *Uncommon Faith* book.

Joanna Cotten was at the end of her rope. She'd exhausted all options. Her lifelong dream of country music stardom was at a crossroads, sidelined by an undiagnosed autoimmune disease. Then one fateful day, Cotten went to see holistic practitioner Felicia McQuaid, the owner of THE Healing Clinic in downtown Fort Walton Beach, FL. A year later, Cotten is filling arenas across the U.S. alongside Eric Church for The Outsiders World Tour.

Joanna is a shining example of the role of faith, healing and transforming the difficult experiences of life in a way that reveals the ultimate divine purpose contained inside of it all.

Hear Joanna's single "Keep My Faith" at: www.uncommonfaithbook.com

To learn more about Joanna visit: www.joannacotten.com

About the Author

Felicia McQuaid, energy specialist, transformational healer, speaker, spiritual counselor and author, unravels the untold stories of her painful past in a transformational journey of *Uncommon Faith*. Uncommon faith is the path of transforming the difficulty of the past to reveal the divine purpose of your past and the purpose of your life in the here and now.

McQuaid's electric energy has been rippling through the Emerald Coast for more than a decade. Using the modalities of reiki, yoga and energy work, she has trained, transformed and touched thousands of lives through her work as the owner of THE Healing Clinic of Fort Walton Beach. During this time, she has traveled to share her wisdom as a motivational speaker and teacher. She is a true teacher, leader and inspirational force for all who come in contact with her. She exemplifies what it means to heal and live with divine purpose.

McQuaid's unwavering love and endless support of others makes her healing style comforting and relatable. Drawing on her strong energetic awareness and spiritual power, she helps others to see their own transformational journey. Experiencing firsthand the impact that healing has had in her life, she believes every person has the ability to grow, learn and heal on all levels.

When she's not practicing healing, McQuaid can be found spending time with her family on the sandy white beaches of the beautiful Emerald Coast, practicing yoga or just simply enjoying all the miracles daily life has to offer.

To learn more about Felicia McQuaid or *Uncommon Faith* please visit: www.uncommonfaithbook.com

With faith all things are possible.

Made in the USA
Charleston, SC
27 January 2015